THE HAPPY NEUROTIC

How to use the Bio-computer between your Ears in the search for Happiness

GEOFF GRAHAM

Author of
How to Become the Parent You Never Had
and
It's a Bit of a Mouthful.'

REAL OPTIONS PRESS

First published in Great Britain 1988 by
Real Options Press
Dunsopp House
Lucy Street
Blaydon upon Tyne
NE21 5PU

BRITISH LIBRARY CATALOGUING IN PUBLICATION DATA

Graham, Geoff
The Happy Neurotic : how to use the bio-computer between your ears in the
search for happiness
1. Psychotherapy
1. Title 616.89'14   RC480

ISBN 0 9511951 2 3

Printed by Martin's of Berwick. Sea View Works, Spittal, Berwick upon Tweed.
TD15 1RS

Contents

The Author

Geoff Graham started using hypnosis and then N.L.P. in his dental practice in 1960. He formed the Northern Counties Branch of The British Society of Medical and Dental Hypnosis in 1969. Since this time he has been involved in lecturing and running workshops both in this country and Europe, North and South America Australia and the Far East. In 1972 he was made a Foreign Fellow of the American Society of Clinical Hypnosis. In 1973 while attending The Pan American Congress of Hypnosis in Brazil he was made a Member of Honour at that Conference. In 1974 he was made an Honorary Fellow of the Singapore Society of Clinical Hypnosis. He is a Founder Fellow of The British Society of Medical and Dental Hypnosis and has acted as a National Assessor for the Certificate of Accreditation issued by that society and possesses a Certificate in his own right.

He has spent over a year attending part-time training as a Primal Therapist with the International Society of Primal Therapists organized by the late Dr W. Swartley. Although he is not a hospital consultant both B.U.P.A. and P.P.P. accept Geoff Graham on a consultant basis when patients are referred to him by other Hospital Consultants. He has now treated well over two thousand patients with hypnosis or N.L.P. most of whom have been referred to him. He is also a member of The International Society of Hypnosis.

He feels many patients seeking help with psychological problems get very little beneficial assistance, and has written this book to make the information and experience he has had the privilege to obtain from patients, available both to therapists, but more importantly to the intelligent public, so that they may be in a position to help themselves, with the carefully structured self-help exercises outlined in this book.

Acknowledgments

I would like to offer my sincere thanks to all those who have helped me to produce this book, especially to Elizabeth who was responsible for the editings. My thanks are also due to Brian who taught me to understand a computer without which I would never have written this book. Nor would I have understood the Bio-computer so well, or how to programme it. Mostly, I would like to thank and dedicate this book to my patients, who have taught me more than anyone, both with the theory and treatment outlined in this book. Without them there would be no book.

Introduction

In my first two books I stated that there were only two types of people, the happy neurotic and the unhappy neurotic. Everybody is neurotic. It is impossible to go on the journey of life without being hurt. The purpose of taking that journey, and the purpose of life itself, is to raise our consciousness to a higher plane and become responsible for ourselves. When we succeed in doing so, we free ourselves from the trap of that hurt. We are no longer stuck having to follow that behaviour which only leads us to where we don't want to go, thus relinquishing all chance of happiness.

As soon as we have options, and become free, we are able to go anywhere we want mentally, and so we are much more likely to be happy on the journey of life. When we succeed in doing that through love, we are aware of our real needs and the needs of others and we are able to help everybody to be more happy. Everyone who meets us is lifted with us, which is the very purpose of life.

In my first two books I looked with you at the things that happen on the journey that imprint and condition us into the trap of the unhappy neurotic. I described various exercises to help us break free from that trap. In this book I want to look more deeply at how we weave that trap for ourselves, and what we can do to change the way we think and feel so that we are different. Many people may argue 'but is that being our real selves?' I say to them, **'You can be anything you want when you know how, so why waste time being unhappy when you can be wonderful? When you are being wonderful and happy, that is being as much your real self as when you are unhappy and trapped. Why be the unhappy neurotic when you can be the happy one?'**

Way back in 1641 the French philosopher *René Descartes,*

1

searching for the absolute truth pertaining to the working of the mind, hypothesized that the only truth is **Cogito Ergo Sum [I think therefore I am.]** In 1641 René Descartes, and every body else for that matter, didn't know much about laterality of the mind. They didn't realise that right-handed people usually use the left hemisphere of their brain to think, but at the same time they use their right hemisphere to feel. If René had added one word 'Feel' to 'I think therefore I am,' and made it *I think [and/or] feel therefore I am*, he would still be true today. Therefore if we can help someone to change whatever they think or feel, we change what they are.

Unhappy neurotics have faulty perceptions in the way they reach what they feel, and have no choice about what they feel. They are stuck with a feeling that leads them to be unhappy. Most of the time they play the BLAME GAME which always results in being stuck [see my first book]. *But what they feel, they are.* If they feel unhappy, they are unhappy, whether or not there is anything in real terms to be unhappy about. If they feel pain, they are hurting, whether or not there is anything in real terms to be hurting about. If they feel frightened, they are afraid, whether or not there is anything in real terms to be frightened about. So whatever they feel, they are, and they seem to have no choice about that. How do they do that? We will look at that later.

The psychotic person has faulty perception in both thinking and feeling. That is what makes most other people unhappy about them. What ever they think and feel, however, so far as they are concerned, they are. If they think and feel they are being taken over by invaders from another planet, so far as they are concerned, they are.

Sören Kierkegaard the Danish philosopher, two hundred years after Descartes, said *'Whenever we translate 'What is' into language or thought, there is always a distortion of 'What is''*.

Whatever we think or say or feel we distort by our internal mechanism, [by the way we think or speak or feel], we cannot help distorting 'What is,' so there is no ultimate truth. The process of language, and/or the process of thought distorts 'What is' and we believe the distortion, and the distortion then becomes our truth. Often this truth leads us to be unhappy and trapped. Therefore if we can change the process of language, or the process of thought, we end up with another distorted belief or truth. But if this new distorted truth makes us happy by giving us more options then why waste time with the old process?

Alfred Korzybski, in his book 'Science and Sanity', long before Bandler and Grinder invented the term N.L.P., [Neuro-Linguistic Programming] said, *'Neuro-Linguistics is the study of how our thinking and talking influences our tissues.'* It seems that it is impossible to think or feel without that having an effect on our tissues.

If we accept that what we think and/or feel we are, and language and the process of thought distorts 'What is', then Neuro-Linguistics ends up as the study of how we distort 'What is' and end up what we are. It is also the study of how we can change that process of how we think so that the distortion ends up giving us more options which will make us happier and more comfortable. This book is an attempt to show you how to do just that. It is an attempt to show you how to change what we think and/or feel, therefore we change what we are. Many of the ideas are learned from Bandler and Grinder and others in the N.L.P. field but the patients and case histories quoted in this book are mine. I have changed names and small things about my patients to protect their identity but the treatments are as they were carried out.

Geoff Graham 1988.

CHAPTER 1

How do we process thought?

So what do we do to think? How do we think? What is the process we use to think or feel? It is impossible to think or feel at all without using our senses. Whatever we say or think, we have to create images with our senses to do that. Many people deny that they are making images to think and may say, for instance 'I can't visualise, I can't make pictures in my head.' This is because those people who have difficulty in making pictures in their conscious mind, make pictures in their unconscious mind rather like transparencies, and see right through them, to a concept in their conscious mind, without ever being aware of the unconscious picture. For example, if I ask you what your favourite colour is, you can't tell me what it is without seeing the colour, either in your conscious or unconscious mind. You have to make a picture of the colour, somewhere, before you can tell me what it is. The only way you can identify what colour is, is to see it. You can't feel, [for instance], red. You can't smell red. You can't hear red. You can't taste red. The only way you can know what red is, is by seeing it. Therefore, before you can know that your favourite colour is red, you have to see it. A person who has been blind all their life cannot have a favourite colour. They cannot know what red is.

For another example look now at the part drawing in fig 1. Do you know what the drawing is?

Fig 1.

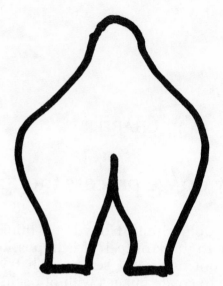

If not look at fig 2. Do you know now what it is?

Fig 2.

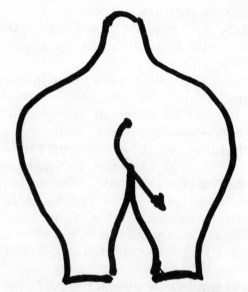

If not look at fig 3. Now everybody knows what it is.

Fig 3.

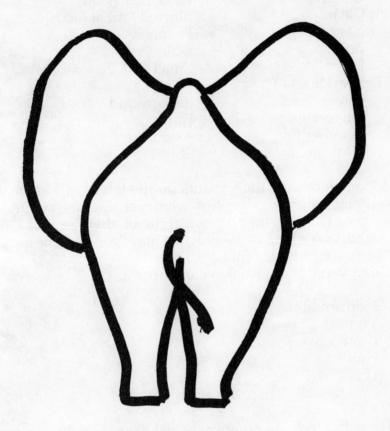

It's an elephant. How do you know it's an elephant and which end of the elephant is it? How do you know which end it is? In order to know the answer to any of these questions you have to complete the picture in your mind, therefore you have to visualise.

Anyone who has not been blind all their life can and does make visual images, either in their conscious, or unconscious, mind, otherwise they wouldn't be able to think about or distinguish any of the following variants of visual perception.

VARIANTS IN VISUAL PERCEPTION

Colour	Black and White
Clear	Blurred [out of focus]
Near	Far away
Bright	Dull
Large	Small
Sparkle	Plain
Foreground	Background
Three dimensional	Flat
Symmetry	Asymmetry
Movement	Still

As a general rule the variants on the left of this list make the thoughts and feelings of whatever you are picturing, stronger. The variants on the right of this list make the thoughts or feelings weaker. There may, however, be quite a few exceptions to this rule.

Other variants of visual perception are:-

Horizontal
Vertical
Perspective
Framed
Unframed

There are always others.

These last five and others may make the thoughts stronger or weaker depending on the individual. All of these variants of visual perception, however, will alter the quality of the images being formed and the thoughts and feelings connected with the images.

It is possible to help people who make transparent pictures in their unconscious mind become aware of them in their conscious mind. The start of this process is to make them accept and know that they do make pictures. With training and acceptance they will begin to see more and more in their conscious. The training consists of asking them to keep on making visual perceptions and at the same time asking them, 'How did you do that?' Eventually they will begin to see the pictures in their conscious mind to a much greater extent.

Many people use Auditory images to think or feel. For instance, many of you, to think, will find yourself talking to yourself in your mind. When you think about it, it is almost impossible to think without talking to yourself. Sometimes you are not consciously aware of talking in your mind before it is pointed out, but when it is, you will find it fascinating to listen to yourself. You may find all sorts of things about yourself and your behaviour that you didn't know before, when you start listening to your thoughts. Just like visual variants there are also Auditory Variants that alter the thoughts and feelings connected with the auditory images.

VARIANTS IN AUDITORY PERCEPTION

Urgent	Peaceful
Compelling	Soft
Noisy	Quiet
Important	Unimportant
Immediate	Later
Persuasive	Boring
Wakeful	Restful
Loud	Hushed
Wild	Gentle
Jarring	Rhythmic
Agitate	Soothing
Laughter	Crying

As a general rule the variants on the left of the above list will make the thoughts and feelings connected with the auditory images stronger, but there are always exceptions. The variants on the right will normally make the thoughts and feelings associated with the auditory images weaker. Once again there are always exceptions.

The most common way to feel something is to make a picture then feel it. V-⟩K But sometimes they say it then feel it A-⟩K. Sometimes to feel something a person will use a combination of the other senses V-⟩A-⟩O-⟩G-⟩K Visual [see]. Auditory [hear]. Olfactory [smell]. Gustatory [taste]. Kinesthetic [feel]. Each sense image can lead on and stimulate another sense image.

Again like the visual and auditory senses there are variants in the Kinesthetic perception that will strengthen or alter the feelings.

VARIANTS IN KINESTHETIC PERCEPTION

Love	Hate
Hot	Cold
Courage	Fear
Pleasure	Discomfort
Glad	Sad
Comfortable	Pressure
Smooth	Rough
Satisfaction	Hunger
Strong	Weak
Still	Movement
Happy	Unhappy
Possess	Loss

There are always others

As a general rule the variants on the left will lead to a more pleasant feeling and the ones on the right will lead to a more unpleasant feeling. Again there are always exceptions.

The Olfactory and Gustatory senses [Smell and Taste] also have variants but the three most important, and frequently used, senses are Visual, Auditory and Kinesthetic. Some smells and tastes, however, do lead to very powerful feelings. E.g. A favourite perfume can have a great effect upon the way a man might feel for a beautiful lady. A warm pint of beer can make a man from the north east of England quite bad tempered. A strong body odour on a man may well be very off putting to a lady.

It is possible, in most people, to tell which senses they are using to make their images, simply by watching them. Therefore it is possible to see how they are processing their thoughts, that is, which senses they are using to process their thoughts. When you know which sense they are using to process thought it is then possible to alter some of the Variants in that sense to change the process of the thought which, if you are skilful, will then end up as a different thought or feeling. If you remember in the Introduction, I said that Rene Descartes said the only truth in the working of the mind is 'I think therefore I am'. By skillfully changing some of Variants in the thought process you will change what a person thinks or feels and therefore you will change what they are.

So how do we recognize which sense a person is using to process what they are thinking? Richard Bandler and John Grinder tell us that we have to look at a person's eyes when they are talking and the way they move their eyes will give us a clue to which sense they are using to process thought. Provided the person is a normally organized right-handed person, if they look upwards or defocus and look straight ahead they are visualizing. You will recognize a person defocusing when their eyes take on a glazed appearance. Bandler and Grinder also tell us that if they are looking up and to the right they are constructing images, and if they look up and to the left they are remembering images. [See fig 4 below].

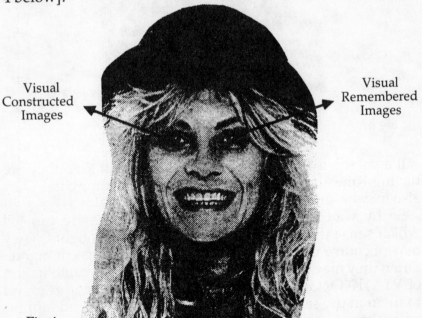

Visual Constructed Images

Visual Remembered Images

Fig 4.

If a person is looking to either side or down to the left, once again Bandler and Grinder tell us that the person is using their auditory sense to process their thoughts. If they are looking to the right then they are constructing sounds or words, and if they are looking to the left they are remembering sounds or words. They are either talking to themselves or listening to sounds. [See fig. 5 below].

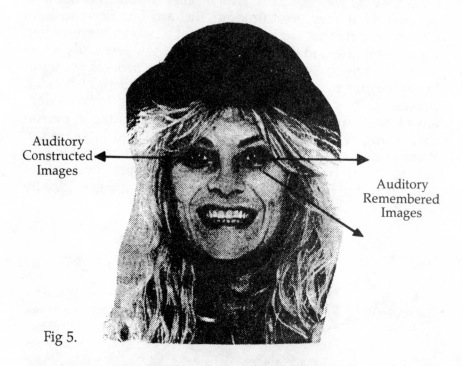

Auditory Constructed Images

Auditory Remembered Images

Fig 5.

If a person is looking down and to the right then they are having Kinesthetic feelings to process their thoughts. They also may be smelling or tasting. [See fig 6 below].

So by watching how they move their eyes we can tell which sense they are using to process their thoughts. They may of course use more than one sense to process thoughts. Often they may go V->K->V->V->K or any other combination of V>A>K<O<G. If, however, you watch them and respond to them in the same sequence you will rapidly build rapport with that person. It is necessary to practice watching a

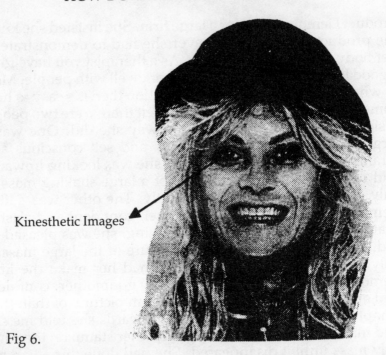

Kinesthetic Images

Fig 6.

person talk to be able to notice and then be able to repeat the sequence. I find one way to practice is to watch the news readers on the television and jot down their sequence of processing. It is always useful to check with a person at the beginning of an interview by asking them a question which will require [let us say] a visual answer. Perhaps, 'How do you see Such and Such?' and watch their eyes. If they look up then you know they visualize by looking up. Check the other senses too. It is always better to check because there are always exceptions to the way people organize their thoughts and move their eyes.

When you have checked and then gone on to gather the information as to how someone is processing their thoughts, by altering some of the listed variants in the senses they are using, it becomes easy to change what they think and feel. For instance Carol came to see me the other day to see if I could help her because she said she found she was shaking all over, particularly when she had to speak in public, and she was afraid she would dry up when talking. She was a

Product Demonstrator for a large firm. She insisted she knew the product well, but whenever she had to demonstrate it, her body would shake all over. As a therapist you have to be a good listener and observer, to work well with people. Most of what you do is to get the information then it's easy to help someone to change. Carol said she felt there were two people inside her making her shake the way she did. One was a large shaking mass of jelly, weak and self conscious and afraid. While she was saying this she was looking upwards and obviously making a picture of a large shaking mass of jelly. She was even shaking slightly. The other was a little demon with horns, tough and cruel, confident and pushy, that made her do it, in spite of shaking, she was pleased he did. Briefly I had her make the picture of the large mass of jelly become much smaller. I also had her make the little demon change into a large kind fairy godmother, confident and encouraging. I had her do a 'Zoom picture' of that. [See Chapter 4 for a Zoom picture]. Afterwards she told me she had made the large kind fairy godmother stamp on the small jelly mass until it disappeared. She had done this all on her own, and now didn't shake any more.

I also asked her about the fear of drying up when she was demonstrating.

She said, 'I just get this fear I will dry up and not be able to say anything when I am talking to the public.'

'When do you first get the fear? Is it before you start to speak?'

'Yes, when I am waiting to go on I just get afraid I will dry up'

'How do you get the fear?'

'I just get it'

'When did you last have it? Go back to that time when you were waiting to go on to demonstrate, shut your eyes so that you can feel you are there. Just before you felt afraid what were you doing?'

'I was telling myself, you might dry up.'

'Why were you doing that? What is telling yourself you might dry up, doing?'

'It's making me feel afraid.'

'Do you want to make yourself afraid?'
'No.'
'Then why tell yourself to be afraid?'
She then said, 'I didn't realize I was, until you showed me what I was doing.'

Most of the time people don't realize what they are doing to themselves. They just programme the bio-computer between their ears automatically, without thinking. When you do that you often end up where you don't want to be.

So we did a 'Zoom auditory picture' of what to say to herself while she was waiting to go on to demonstrate [for Zoom auditory picture see Chapter 4].

I also gave her a new direction for her mind to take her. She had driven herself in her car to see me so I asked her if she could remember what her biggest fear was when she first started to learn to drive.

After some prompting from me she said it was that the **car would run away with her** and perhaps crash into another car, or a wall, or the kerb, or whatever. In other words she wouldn't be in control of the car.

Then I asked her if she remembered the day when she had just taken her test and was sitting in the car with the test instructor, and he gave her the piece of paper that said she had passed her test.

She smiled and looked up and said, 'Yes.' She didn't need to tell me, I knew she remembered by her smile and I also knew she really felt good about passing her test. As she also looked upwards I also knew she had just made a picture of the piece of paper that said she had passed, even though it was many years since she had taken her test. I asked her if passing meant she was now able to drive the car where she wanted and not where the car wanted to go.

She smiled again and I knew her answer before she said, 'Yes.'

People always show externally what they are thinking on the inside, so it is very important to watch them when you are talking with them. Sometimes what they show on the outside doesn't correspond to what they are actually saying, and you know there is a conflict somewhere in their mind. It is very important to notice this conflict as it will need resolving if the person is to make a change in what they think.

I asked her if she was to drive home by taking every second left turn on the road, how long would it take her to get home. She seemed puzzled, so I repeated, **'Yes every second left turn, would you get home at all?'**

After a while she said, 'I would be going round in circles.'

'Yes' I said, **'You would. You would never get home if you let the car take every second left turn.'**

'How long do you think it would take you to get home if you started the car up and then got into the back seat and let the car drive you where ever it wanted to go?' She again looked puzzled.

'I would never get home. The car can't drive itself.'

I said, **'You know most people spend more time learning to drive a car, or a washing machine, or a computer, or even a one-armed bandit, than they spend learning to drive their own minds. If you don't drive your own mind it will most probably take you somewhere you don't want to go. Or even worse, someone else will drive it where you don't want to go.'**

She laughed, [it always works better if the patient laughs]. 'You mean I have been letting my mind run me instead of me running my mind?'

'It sounds that way to me,' I said, **'How would it feel if I give you a piece of paper that says you have now passed your mind driving test?'**

She smiled and said, 'That would be fantastic.'

I asked her to picture herself with that piece of paper that said she had just passed her mind driving test and she shut her eyes and smiled again. I knew she could see it so I didn't need to ask. She had just given her mind a new direction to go in. She had told it she was now in the driving seat and she felt good about that. I had her do a 'Zoom picture' of that. [See Chapter 4].

Another example of how important it is to drive your own mind, and not let it drive you, happened to me on 1st August 1986. On 2nd August '86 my daughter was getting married and on the evening before, my wife and I were having a party with some friends and relatives who had come to Newcastle for the wedding the next day. About 9. p.m. my niece came to our house and said with great alarm that she thought my wife's shop was on fire. She had just passed, on her way to the house and a fire engine and the police were all round the shop. My wife and I went to the shop and found my consulting rooms, which were next door to the shop, were alight, with smoke pouring out of all the windows. Her shop was not on fire.

The police and firemen said my rooms were completely gutted but the fire was now out. The police said it looked like arson. They had found some spent matches in a cupboard and it looked as if the fire had been started deliberately. They said it was still too smoky and dangerous for me to go into the building but they had sent for a firm who would board up the burned windows and doors to make it secure. They suggested that I should just go home as there was nothing I could do tonight and they would contact me sometime tomorrow. I informed them that my daughter was getting married the next day so they said they would leave it until 3rd. August. My wife and I went home and finished the party and went to bed and to sleep. I had to talk very softly to myself to get to sleep and awoke about 6.30 a.m. My first thoughts were [I could hear myself saying to myself] 'I wonder if the firemen or police have turned off the gas main and electricity. They didn't ask me where the main was. The central heating is due to come on at 8.30 a.m. and the gas pipe may be damaged and the electricity may spark and the whole building may blow up'. I got dressed and returned to the surgery and found to my surprise that the gas and electricity mains were both still on. I turned them off and as it was now daylight I picked my way through the building. The whole place was black and burned out. Everything seemed completely ruined. People who saw it on the Monday morning said they couldn't have imagined it as bad as it was. In the end there was about £40,000 worth of damage. There seemed nothing more I could do so I just went home.

As I was going home I reminded myself that today was my

daughter's wedding day and I began to make pictures of the wedding. I associated with all the wedding thoughts and dissociated from all the fire thoughts. So much so that when I arrived at the church with my daughter and the Canon who was performing the wedding ceremony met us at the church entrance, and said, 'So sorry to hear your bad news', I thought briefly he was unable to marry my daughter. That was the only bad news that was going to affect me today. I asked him why he couldn't marry her, and he said, 'No, your fire'. I just said, 'No problem, let's get on with the wedding'. I think he thought I was a little light in the head. I suppose I was light in the head as I had been making very pleasant pictures about one of the best days in my daughter's life. The wedding went off very well indeed. My wife and I and all the guests enjoyed the day immensely, as did my daughter and her husband. The fire was another day.

I had a patient today [the day I wrote this chapter] who, when I was explaining the theory about who is driving his mind and said, 'If you don't drive it, it will either drive itself at random and probably end up where you don't want to be, or, even worse, someone else will drive it', said, 'You're right, my wife is driving me mad.' He wasn't speaking, as he thought, metaphorically, he literally was saying his wife was driving his mind to where he didn't want to go.

CHAPTER 2

How to create the right conditions for change

Before you can change the way someone thinks or feels so that you change what they are, you have to have the right conditions to make that change. Many people are so entrenched in their trap that they think they will never get out. Remember 'I think therefore I am'. If they think they can't change, it is going to be more difficult to change them. This pessimism on the patient's part is often caused by previous unsuccessful attempts at change, unfortunately very often reinforced by the wrong treatment. Sometimes this resistance to change is caused by a desperately weakened 'EGO' with the person hanging on like grim death to whatever they are, afraid if they let go they will disintegrate into hell. Most of my patients have been everywhere before they end up with me. Nothing has worked before. Some of them have even been told to go and live with it. Some have been told that there is no cure for their complaint. Unfortunately there are a lot of therapists and people in the helping professions who don't know a great deal about changing people. This is the main reason I am writing this book. I hope it will both stimulate the professionals to learn some more and give some people, who have no hope, a chance to grasp a glimpse of light at the end of the tunnel. No therapist can cure everyone, nor does any therapy cure everything, but if one can't, perhaps there is someone, or something else, that may succeed. Many patients are resistant to change as a defence against disappointment. They have been disappointed so many times before.

The most essential condition for change is RAPPORT, by which I mean the close relationship and understanding between therapist and patient. The next is the ability to communicate both ways. The therapist must be able to communicate with the person requiring help, but equally important is the patient's ability to communicate with the therapist. A prerequisite of change is the therapist's knowledge of the process of change, and his or her natural ability to understand the problem. It does not necessarily follow that someone with a lot of letters after their name knows how to change people better than somebody else. Being brilliant academically doesn't always mean you are a good therapist. Remember there are a lot of people in the help game who are there for the wrong reasons. There are a lot of con artists about in the help business. If you, as a person, don't feel comfortable with your therapist, or if you are getting no help, then think about a change of therapist or treatment.

So how do you establish Rapport? Most of all, rapport is built on matching behaviour. If a patient is making visual images, [and you should be able to tell which senses they are using by looking at their eye movement] it won't build rapport if you ask them how they feel about that without first using a visual statement. If you want to change the sense image a person is using you must first answer them in the same sense, then change the sense. For example, if a person is talking about any of the visual variants on the list in Chapter 1 and you want to change their perception to Kinesthetic [Feelings], you should say something like. 'So that's how you see it, but how do you feel about it?' This helps to make a smooth change from one sense to another. This smooth change of sensual representation will actually produce a state of waking hypnosis where the person is paying more attention to you and is distracted much less. Hypnosis is any effective communication where a person is narrowing their field of attention and concentrating more within that field. It is always wise to follow a person's way of thinking first.

If a person is talking about one of their beliefs, it will not build rapport if you disagree in the beginning. You will only switch them off listening. Later, when you have established rapport, you can change beliefs, see Chapter 6. Talking too fast or talking down to someone won't build rapport. If the person can't hear you, either because you are talking too softly, or because they are a little hard of hearing, rapport won't be established.

If you say something the patient doesn't want to agree with, or understand, that won't establish rapport. First you have to give the patient a reason to believe in whatever you want to say and they always have to understand you. Remember, it is the patient who is going to make the change, so if they don't understand what you are talking about, they can't make any change that is going to be of any use.

Pace the patient by gauging the tempo of your voice and your breathing, to the rate of their breathing. [Pace means copy, at the same rate]. When you have paced the patient try leading them. Alter the rate of your breathing and talking and see if they follow. If they do, rapport is established. If they don't, you must pace them a little longer. When rapport is firmly established they will follow your lead.

Use transitional words to join your sentences, so that your speech seems to be flowing smoothly from one thing to the next. Words like the ones below make a smooth flow in the conversation.

Transitional words.
As, when, and, but, while, even as, so, and there are always others. These words join sentences easily and keep the chain of thought moving smoothly along, so there is no break in the thought process. This stops the person injecting doubts of their own in the pauses, because the transitional words cut out the pauses.

It is essential to watch, very carefully, the person you are talking with. They will respond, externally, to the things you are saying and the things they are feeling, inside. [See the first chapter about the lady passing her driving test and mind driving test]. You may be talking with someone and saying something which, to you, is perfectly innocent and non-emotive, but to the person, what you are saying may be very emotive. Watch and notice what is happening inside the other person otherwise you will lose rapport. If you want to produce a positive response you should be able to detect it externally. If you don't, either you have not been looking [which is fatal if you want to work with someone], or it isn't having the desired effect. If they are talking about something bad, with a smile on their faces you know they are defending against the feelings and their talking and feelings are incongruous.

Using indirect suggestions is often much more powerful than saying something straight out. An example, I sometimes use, if I want to use hypnosis, is tell someone, who is about to sit down, to not go into trance before they sit down. This is indirectly telling them to go into trance when they do sit down, and if you then do nothing the patient will often go into trance as they don't know what else to do. Using metaphor is also a useful way of making indirect suggestions to the unconscious mind. When you are telling a story a person's unconscious mind will often pick out from what you have been saying exactly what it wants. This may not be what you have actually been saying, but what their unconscious mind wanted to hear. It is always useful to examine what you said once before, and see if you could have implied the same thing without actually coming out with it. Then you have a useful way of saying it next time. Often patients will respond more strongly to this form of communication because they think they thought of it themselves.

If you want someone to do, or think, something, you must notice things about them and tell them about those facts which they can verify as correct. Having said, perhaps, three or more correct verifiable facts slip in what you want the person to believe next; and having just said, internally, 'Yes, yes, yes,' the person is more likely to say 'Yes' again, and make what you wanted to happen actually happen next. This is again leading them into where you want them to go either in thought or behaviour. For instance, if the person is sitting looking at you and smiling and at the same time they are looking upwards [making internal pictures in their head] you could say, 'As you are sitting there you obviously **see** what I am saying is **amusing [pleasing,** depending on content], so perhaps you would [or could,—or may,—find that,—be] more relaxed by closing your eyes'. [Or what ever you want to happen next].

There are various things that may lose rapport and set up a resistance to change. With all these things it is the therapist's job to find a way round the resistance. It is necessary to change the way you are communicating with the patient if resistance is present. You should be able to notice resistance in the external behaviour of the patient. They may become tense, or fidget, or do the opposite to what you are saying, or just look uncomfortable. The reasons for resistance are manifold, and some of them are listed below.

Reasons for Resistance.
   Inadequate Motivation
   Errors of Ambiguity
   Failure to understand a request
   Fear of Submission to your wishes
   Fear of Failure to make the change
   Incompatibility of thinking
   Defiance of Authority, or Hostility towards the therapist
   Inability to Concentrate
   Fear of loss of symptoms
   There are always others.

To facilitate change in grossly neurotic persons, or very unhappy people, it is often useful to establish some positive anchors to help the patient have a better self image, and to become more receptive to the idea of change, or even the possibility of change. In other words to build their 'Ego'. To do this, have them go over a past memory when their behaviour was more confident [happy, efficient, relaxed] and see if you can strengthen the feelings connected with that memory by altering some of the variants in the way they process the memory. [See Chapter 4]. Some grossly unhappy people who are hopelessly stuck in their behaviour find it very difficult to remember anything in their past that was positive. This is where it is necessary to prompt them into a positive memory. Everybody went through conception so this is where I find my explanation of the 'Marathon', they swam to be here, is useful. [See my book 'How To Become The Parent You Never Had']. Nobody can argue they didn't go through it. The success depends on how you tell the story of it.

EXERCISE 1

I tell my patients that I am going to tell them a true story of something that happened to them, long ago, that they have forgotten about. In order to concentrate on the story I suggest that they might like to close their eyes by turning their eyes upwards and keeping them turned up, just close their lids [Spiegel's eye closure, hypnotic induction]. I then tell them to relax their eyes to the point where they won't open and at that point turn their mind inwards to concentrate on the story. [Elman's deepening plus N.L.P.].

Then I say to them 'You know a long time ago you were released in the birth canal with fifty million other sperm and the size you were and the distance you had to travel was equivalent to you now running a marathon race'. I suggest they might like to imagine this marathon as a movie film in colour. 'Make it brighter and clearer and very real, because it did happen. See yourself clearly as the one in front, the one leading the others to the ovum. I know the sperm is only half of you but it was the active half of you. [For Females: and it carried the sex gene to the ovum, and your sperm was all female and it beat millions of male sperm]. See it do that now, clearly and courageously winning all the way. And when you reach the ovum you were the one that entered the ovum and created your life. See yourself doing that now, and feel it'. [V->K procedure, >see -> feel} also changing representational systems to deepen the hypnotic procedure.]

'Tell yourself, as you created your own life, you asked to be here. Tell yourself clearly and proudly [A->K >talk -> feel} procedure deepening hypnotic induction] that as there is no-one else on this earth for any other reason than that, you have just as much right as anyone else to be here. Feel how that feels, feel it strongly, feel it with pride, with satisfaction. Tell yourself that you have already proved you are fit enough to take the journey of life and succeed. Tell yourself that the purpose of life is to free yourself from the traps that stop you being happy and raise your consciousness to a higher plane where you are responsible for yourself, and you have already proved that you are the fittest of fifty million to do that. Now hang on to all those feelings with all your strength [A-)K]. See that the very purpose of life is to make those necessary changes to free one's self from the traps one creates, and have more options'. [V-)K]

'Following that marathon you started a journey through life. Various things happened to you on that journey which taught you behaviours and how to modify the way you think and feel. But the way you think and feel you learned, so you can learn to modify how you think and feel and then you can be different. Many of your behaviours are no longer relevant to your circumstances now, but your brain is still doing them, randomly, in an attempt to help you. You must run your brain the way you want it to go and I will show you how. When you do, your life will be happier and you will have more options in everything you do'.

'You will free yourself from playing the 'Blame Game'. The blame game is where you blame others, or other things, for how you feel. A feeling is a personal experience which you manufacture for yourself. Fear is such a feeling. If you start blaming others, or other things for your fear, then the only way out of your fear is for others, or other things, to change. As others, or other things, are unlikely to change you become trapped with your fear. Other feelings are the same. It is the way you manufacture, or process, your feelings or thoughts that makes you unhappy or uncomfortable. When you learn other ways to process your thoughts and feelings you will become far happier and much more comfortable. This is taking charge of running your brain and the purpose of life'. [See my first book **'How to become the parent you**

never had' and the purpose of life is to become responsible for yourself].

In order to make it possible for someone to change we have to know at least two things. First we have to know how someone is processing their thoughts and/or feelings. Then we have to know what they **would like to think or feel.** So we need to find out how the bio-computer between the ears is programmed in the first place, and then how to change the programming to get what you want. The more acceptable the end programme is to the patient, the more the brain will find ways to change the programme when it is shown how. It is the 'patient's want power', that will make the programming easier.

CHAPTER 3

The trap
How not to use your mind

The first thing we have to do, when we are helping someone to change what they think or feel, is to find out how they process what they want to change. What we want to change are those processes that make them do things they don't want to do, or those things that make them unhappy or uncomfortable. That means we have to find out what programme is in the bio-computer that we must change.

First of all it must be easy and quick to learn a new process. If it wasn't, it wouldn't be so easy to learn negative processes that result in being 'stuck'. People wouldn't be so expert at being 'stuck'. Many ordinary people seem to have an enormous ability at being 'stuck' and doing things they don't want to do, over and over again.

I believe all phobias are imprinted learned behaviours. They are all 'one off' learned experiences. One moment the person is perfectly normal, and the next, they are phobic. The experience, that made them phobic, may have been a really traumatic experience, or may even have just been imagined. Something may have triggered off a thought ->feeling, [V->K or A->K]. Something that had been triggered off from the past, that had nothing to do in real terms with whatever was going on currently, but nevertheless from there on in, the person is programmed to react in a certain way. They didn't even realize how, or that they themselves had made the programme but they become stuck with it. They blame the circumstances, or whatever was happening at the time, for how they feel, never realizing or accepting it was they who programmed the bio-computer between their ears. They play the 'Blame Game' and hence are stuck with it. For instance someone with a lift phobia may have actually been stuck in a lift when it broke down and thereafter been afraid of lifts. They make repeat pictures in their mind of the lift breaking down, and them being stuck in it all over again, every time they have to get in a lift. V.->K. But another way of developing a lift phobia, probably much more common than the way mentioned above, is for someone travelling in a lift to suddenly imagine a picture of the lift breaking down and them being stuck, or suffocating because it broke down, or they picture themselves not being able to get out. This process of imagining they would be trapped forces them to make birth pictures in their mind, thus scaring the living daylights out of themselves. From there on, they repeat the same pictures every time they are in a lift, blaming the lift, when in real terms, the lift had nothing to do with making the pictures. It just happened to be the place where someone let their mind drive them to where they didn't want to be, but by blaming the lift they are stuck with the phobia. Many other behaviours are also imprinted in the same way. How do they do it? Exactly as I have explained above, but first let us look at other ways of how not to use your mind.

Have you ever dreaded anything? Something that hasn't even happened yet? Something in the future that in real terms, may or may not be bad. If you dread it, you have made it bad even before it has happened. You have put a programme in the bio-computer that will make it bad no matter what. The Dental phobic is just such a person. They make their dental treatment bad, even before they get to the dentist, by programming themselves. Then they blame the dentist, or what he has to do, for their fear. Whatever the dentist does then will be bad, it's already been programmed to be so by the patient. [See in the chapter on phobias the treatment for a dental phobic. She didn't even realize she was programming herself, to make her phobic]. In fact all phobics do that, they make themselves afraid before the event, so naturally when it happens, they nearly frighten themselves to death.

If you let your brain run wild you are stuck with it. If you don't take responsibility for your feelings, and you blame outside influences for how you feel, and you have programmed those outside influences to be bad, then you are well and truly stuck. You don't even realize it's you who has done all that to yourself. Unfortunately most people spend more time and effort learning how to use any household appliance than they spend learning to use their own mind to change something and make themselves happier.

Have you ever been haunted by fears or thoughts? Have you never said 'I wish I could forget it'? Have you never said 'I can't do that,' even before you have tried. With people who say, 'I can't do that,' a therapist has to change this belief before he/she can help anyone make good changes in their lives. You have to have a tremendous ability to be so negative. You seem to be able to forget all sorts of things but when it comes to something you are afraid of, or some powerful thought that prevents you from doing something you want to do, you show sheer genius in being able to remember it every time. Thus you condemn yourself to unhappiness. How do you do it? You programme yourself to be like that without even knowing it, and if you made the programme you can change it when you know how. Your brain has shown it works perfectly by being so negative, you just gave it the wrong programme to work on. When you know how, you can be any damn thing you want that is possible for any other average human being. All you have to do is put the right programme in the bio-computer between your ears.

I was working with a man the other day, helping him to make some changes in his behaviour and he said, 'When I find I am not doing what I want to do I think of my forehead like my car radio and cassette player, and I press my forehead between my eyes and I imagine I take out the unwanted cassette, then I put a new one in, and I do what I want. The area between the eyes looks a little like a cassette player in the car so that is how I change my programme.' I had shown him a number of ways to change the way he thought, he just added this one for himself. When people begin to see they can change, they find all sorts of interesting ways of doing that for themselves. The man I was helping used to dread having to meet anyone face to face. He was alright talking to someone on the phone but if he had to meet in person he just went blank and couldn't say anything. He would avoid personal meetings and then get all worked up with himself afterwards. Now he is going towards such meetings, instead of walking away from them. I taught him by dreading them he was programming himself to avoid them. His mind worked perfectly, he told it he was afraid of personal meetings so his mind helped him to avoid them. As soon as he stopped dreading such meetings he was much more able to say what he wanted, person to person, without fear.

Have you ever thought that you loved someone, only to find after a little while you began to feel you had changed and didn't love them anymore. You hadn't changed, only the way you thought about the other person had changed. Falling in love is a temporary state of insanity. Falling out of love is also a temporary state of insanity. It is all too easy for a couple to meet and fall in love. To do this they see all good in each other and no bad, thus they are temporarily insane. They are only half conscious about each other. They get married and all too often something makes them do the reverse. They see all bad in each other and no good. Once again they are in a temporary state of insanity. They are once again only half conscious about the way they see each other. They say we have changed so we may as well get divorced. They haven't changed, only the way they think about each other has changed. If there are children involved, if both partners are willing I am convinced that by helping both partners it is always possible to get both of them into a better relationship than they ever had, even before they fell out. What every child needs, ideally, is two parents who love each other and show it. The child also needs both parents to love him/her and show it. I am convinced that all both parents need to do, is to reprogramme both of their minds to do that. To do this they need therapy, not guidance. Unfortunately most people in the marriage help business don't know how to change people. [See Chapter 5].

Helen came to see me because she had fallen in love with a schizophrenic young man called Brian. He was very disturbed and led poor Helen a merry dance. One minute he would say he loved her and the next he would say she was useless and couldn't do anything right. He would say he admired Helen and with the next breath he would say she wouldn't ever be any use at anything. Poor Helen didn't know what to think. Her beliefs in herself, because of this schizophrenic young man, nearly drove her crazy. She let him drive her mind. If you don't drive your own mind someone else will, and more often than not they will drive you where you don't want to be. That's no way to find happiness. Helen certainly wasn't happy. Brian kept threatening to leave her. He made her pregnant, then left her and told her he didn't ever want to see her again. She didn't know what to do, then after accepting advice from many sources and conscious of the fear that the baby may inherit schizophrenia, she decided after much soul searching to have an abortion. By this time she felt she couldn't bring the baby up by herself and Brian didn't want to know Helen at all. She really could do nothing else.

Brian then successfully committed suicide. Helen felt she was to blame, she should have saved him somehow. I don't know how, you can't stop someone doing that if they have decided that is what they are going to do. It certainly wasn't Helen's fault. Brian had told someone that if Helen had kept the baby it would have given him something to live for. What rubbish! If he really thought that why didn't he tell Helen? Why did he leave her all alone to decide? Why did the other person then tell Helen that is what he said? Some people do the craziest things to other human beings. [See Chapter 5. On abuse]. It was just before Brian's suicide and after the abortion that Helen came to see me. She felt terribly guilty about the abortion, and even worse after the suicide. She felt the only way out was for her to kill herself. Her beliefs about herself, which were totally unfounded, because they were programmed by someone else, made her think of suicide as a way out.

She thought she couldn't live without Brian. There was nothing to live for without him. [She kept making negative images that made her feel ⟩V-⟩K A-⟩K⟩ that there was no point in life without him, in spite of the fact that when she had been with him life was hell]. It just goes to show that being in love is a state of temporary madness, you only notice the good, and allow someone else to programme your mind. She felt useless as Brian had told her she was, and she hadn't prevented him from killing himself so she must be useless. How crazy can you get?

It took me quite a time to stop Helen making these negative pictures, and saying all these negative things to herself. You can see while she was doing the things in the previous paragraph to herself, her life wasn't worth living. She was programming it that way. She was so busy feeling bad, she had no energy to get well. After a while though, by changing some of her beliefs about herself, I was able to stop her programming herself that way, and she began to pick up her life again. It was all the more difficult because she didn't want to think ill of Brian. She wanted to remember the good things about him, otherwise her love was just false.

She asked me 'I must know if Brian 'Really' loved me. Did he?' I just reminded her that when someone was in love they were in a temporary state of insanity and when they were falling out of love they were also insane. In between those states they, hopefully, love you. When someone loves you, some of the time they think about you very fondly and some of the time they don't. There is no such thing as 'Really' loving someone. Part of the time, when he was being nice he loved her, then when he wasn't being nice he didn't. I went to explain that I love my wife. Part of the time I think she is fantastic, but then other times she drives me up the wall. See what I am saying, I sometimes allow her to drive my mind where I don't want to be. I am sure she thinks the same way about me. Fortunately for both of us and our children we love each other more of the time. There is no such state on earth where someone is permanently in love with someone else, outside of an asylum. Love is not a permanent state, it varies from time to time. Helen is now getting on with her life and finding more ways to be happy. She has changed many of her programmes that resulted in her being 'stuck' being unhappy.

Have you, or any of your friends, had a partner who has been unfaithful? You, or your friend, have found out about it and the affair is ended. Your [or your friend's], partner has told you it is all over and they don't really know why they did it and they wish they hadn't had the affair. You still love them and they love you. But you can't let go of it, you can't let it be over. You are blind with jealousy. You keep throwing it at your partner until they leave. You end up hating yourself for your stupid behaviour. It was your partner who was unfaithful but you end up hating yourself. How do you do that? There are five ways you do that in this paragraph, five ways you are stuck.

1. You can't let go of it. You either make pictures or tell yourself about not letting go. [V->K A->K]
2. You can't let it be over. You either make pictures or you tell yourself it's still happening, even when you know it isn't. [V->K A->K].
3. You are blind with jealousy. You won't see the good things about your partner, you are deliberately blind to them. [V->K].
4. You picture, or tell yourself to throw it at your partner, even when they don't want it. [V->K A->K].
5. You make pictures or tell yourself of how hateful you really are and you won't stop even when it hurts only you. [V->K A->K]. There are always other ways to do stupid things. When you know what they are you can reprogramme the bio-computer between your ears and be different. You can be any damn thing you want when **YOU** drive your mind.

I was helping a lady who found out her husband was having an affair when she found a letter in the pocket of his suit which she was taking to the cleaners. She confronted him and he admitted it, but swore it was over. They both loved each other and wanted to be together. She believed him but she kept on seeing that letter in her head. [V->K]. She was letting a letter drive her mind. I had to help her picture something else because she was 'stuck' with the letter. [See slide change in Chapter 4].

I was helping another lady who had found out her husband had had an affair and like the last one, the affair was over and dead. She kept on seeing her husband in bed with the other girl [V->K] and lots of other crazy things that he may have done in the past but wasn't doing now. She just wouldn't let it be over. She got depressed and upset and hated herself [told herself she was being awful. A->K which made her very unhappy] and just about drove him away by her violent behaviour towards him even when she insisted she still loved and wanted him. She was advised to separate from him, by the marriage guidance do-gooders, which really was the last thing she wanted to do. We [she and I] were able to help her to make better images which helped her to stay where she wanted to be [with her husband]. [See slide change in Chapter 4].

Have you any children who you want to trust and communicate with, but you can't trust or communicate with them without insulting them? Human insult creates self-destruct mechanisms. You love your children but you end up making them hate you. How do you do that? [See Chapter 5. on Abuse].

Currently, with the enormous increase in publicity of child abuse, we should look at how someone who has been abused should not use their minds so that they are constantly unhappy. Also we need to look at how the authorities, in response to the abuse accusation, by only paying attention to their own internal pictures, have in many cases abused the children far worse than the original abuse, even if it did take place. Most of the abused, in later life, when the abuse has long since stopped, display a wide range of psychological disturbances. Many of them are depressed or even suicidal. Many have a tremendous feeling of guilt, or feel dirty, or are sexually repressed. Many end up abusing their own children or have a wish to hurt their children in some way. [For examples see Chapter 5]. How do they do that when they were the innocent party?

How many of you have inhibiting compulsions which play havoc with your lives? How many of you keep putting dried up leaves, wrapped round with paper, into your mouths, then you set the leaves alight and draw air over those burning leaves so that the smoke goes down your throat to kill you. You protest you don't want to die and you wish to stop smoking, yet you keep on putting the cigarettes into your mouth and lighting them. Jack came for help because he had been into hospital and lost half of his lung, already, with cancer. He was still smoking about 20 to 40 cigarettes a day. He couldn't work any more because he couldn't stop coughing while he smoked. He protested he wanted to live and his family were all on to him to stop smoking because they said they loved him and didn't want him to die. He said he wanted to stop smoking yet he kept putting one cigarette in his mouth after another and lighting them. How does he do that? [See Chapter 5. Abuse of self].

How many of you want to lose weight, yet you secretly stuff all sorts of food into your mouth when no-one is looking and you protest you haven't eaten anything? How do you do that? How does an alcoholic say he must stop drinking when he pours alcohol down his or her throat whenever he can?

How does anyone do any compulsive behaviour when they protest they don't want to do it?

How does anyone have difficulty in getting angry when they have good cause to be furious? I have had to help many people who had just cause to be angry, who instead of showing their anger to the person responsible for making them uncomfortable, bottled it up inside themselves causing all sorts of ailments, or even worse, taken it out on their loved ones after the event, just like the old song 'You always hurt the one you love, the one you shouldn't hurt at all.' How and why do they do that?

How does a dental phobic remember to be terrified every time they go to the dentist? They are able to forget all sorts of other things but they never forget to be afraid of the dentist, even when the dentist is a very nice, friendly person. All phobics seem to be able to remember to be afraid when they enter their phobic situation. They were, very easily, able to learn to be afraid of their phobia with a one trial learning experience and then for the rest of their lives they are able to remember to be be frightened again and again and again. Even when the next time the circumstances may be really different. How do they do that? [See in Chapter 7, Treatment of dental phobic and doctor phobia].

Have you ever had to do something you weren't particularly keen on doing, and said to yourself or someone else 'I hate doing that'? If you have to do something it is always better to find a way of enjoying doing it before you start. If you hate doing it you just make it all the more unpleasant and difficult to do. Why do you that? and how do you make it worse? You either make hateful pictures of doing it or you tell yourself that you hate doing it. [V->K A->K]. Either of these two things will make your perception of doing it negative and you end up being unhappy. I was helping a lady today who is always anxious and depressed and she said 'Now and then I have a good day but it never lasts more than one day.'

I asked her **'What happens the next day to spoil it?'** and pressed her for an answer.

She said 'I don't know, I get up in the morning and say to myself 'How on earth did I manage to be so well yesterday?' How will I ever keep it up?' [A->K].

I asked to repeat what she had just said in exactly the same way as she had just told me the first time. Then when she had done that, I repeated it back to her in exactly the same tone and emphasis and asked her to interpret the meaning of what she was saying to herself.

She said 'I won't be able to keep it up, being well, will I?' So her mind just did exactly what she had programmed it do do. It made her feel bad again. [She had plenty of negative images of being bad to rely on]. She really was expert at making herself have a bad day.

How does someone, trying to get to sleep, manage to toss and turn all night and hardly get any sleep? Or how does someone who has to get up at a certain time, manage to think only of how much longer they can sleep when it is time to get up? I remember recently when I was giving a workshop in Glasgow on a Sunday, I went up to Glasgow on Saturday afternoon. I checked into my hotel, and was met by one of the organizing committee, and taken out to dinner, and was well wined and dined as is the Scottish custom. Afterwards I was taken back to my hotel late at night and went to bed. Luckily [because I heard myself and knew how to do something about it, often you don't and just are stuck in a behaviour] as I lay down in my bed I heard myself say to myself 'I will never sleep in this bed it's too soft.' [A-)K]. I had had some back trouble years ago and solved it by getting a hard bed to sleep on. My back has been trouble free since getting this orthopaedic bed. I thought 'you stupid idiot' when I realized what I had just said to myself in the hotel room in Glasgow. There was only one bed in the room and it was too late to ask for another room as the reception desk was no longer open. I got out of bed and walked round the room and as I approached the bed I said both outside and inside my head 'Ah! this bed looks much better, I'm sure I will be able to sleep in this one.' I got back into the same bed and went straight to sleep and woke about one minute before the alarm went off the next morning. If I hadn't done what I did, I'm sure I would have tossed and turned all night. I had to get up out of bed to do this, it was too late by the time I had said what I said, to be able to persuade myself while I still lay there. Once you are in a thing [programmed up and running] it's very difficult to change the programme while it's still running. You have to pre-programme yourself for sometime in the future. Getting out of bed ended the old programme, so I was able then to reprogramme myself for when I got back into the bed and it worked. My back felt good, too, in the morning and I believe my workshop was very successful.

I remember when I first started writing books, I bought myself what I thought was an expensive computer to help me. Friends who had written books all told me you must get a computer, it's much easier to write when you do. When I was learning to use the computer it seemed impossible to get it to do the things I wanted. I used to shout and curse the damn thing, then when I realized it would only do what it was programmed to do it seemed much easier to understand. Brains [Bio-computers—living computers] are like that. They will only do what they are told to do. People work perfectly, they may not like what they do, but they are able to do it over and over again until they drive themselves crazy. It's just the programme that is wrong. It is the way YOU [or worse still someone else] programmes YOUR bio-computer that drives you crazy. It's not some outside force, or something you can't help, you have just used the wrong programme. When you spend a little time learning to programme yourself you can do anything you want, just like learning to use a computer. You must want to change. It is how much better you would like to be the changed person that makes it all possible. It is very difficult to make someone do something they don't want to do when they know what they are doing, they have to want to change. They have to be able to see [Make a picture in their Bio-computer] how much more they would like themselves as the changed person.

I was helping a boxer who had lost a fight in front of his home crowd through his over-confidence. He had thought, 'I can finish this fight anytime so I will show them what I can do', and instead of finishing it, he got hit himself. He was so surprised by this, he froze and got hit again. He had learned from this to freeze in the ring during a fight. You can imagine what happened to him when he froze in the ring. At worst he got knocked out, at best he lost the fight. Anyhow we quickly got him over this by having him do a split screen exercise [see next chapter for split screen technique]. He quickly began winning again. He was in for a commonwealth championship title fight and he came to see me for a boost to help him win the fight. I asked him how differently he would see himself as the commonwealth champion. He said he would really have made it then. At least it would be the first step to something great. As he said it you could see a smile of pleasure all over his face. I knew he could really see it inside his mind. That is all I needed to know. I did a 'slide change' with him [see description of slide change in the next chapter] and he said afterwards that the room looked brighter. The room was the same, but how he was seeing it, as the commonwealth champion, was brighter, so I knew what we had done had worked.

As I write this book he is the current Commonwealth and British champion at his weight. After his fight, at a radio interview, he said he had had to go deeper into his mind to win than ever before. I wondered if he quite [literally] knew what he was saying. I knew. He just made the right pictures to win, he deserved to win as he was now running his own mind. He said, 'It will take a lot now to get this title off me' and he meant it, he was still making good pictures. He has gone on to spar with Tyson and I wish him luck in the future and good images. He deserves good luck, he has spent time learning to drive his mind, which is just as important as learning to box. [Or to do any sport].

CHAPTER 4

The techniques for change

So how do we programme the bio-computer between your ears so that you think differently, therefore you are different? Just as Descartes said 'I think therefore I am,' if what you think is different then you are different. This is the whole secret behind changing people. There are many ways to change a person, but there is no way that will change everyone. Neither is there any therapist who will change everyone. Therapy is about two people working together to create changes. It is possible for many people to work with themselves to create changes once they know how. This book is an attempt to show you how.

1. Story telling as a way to make changes

Psychotherapy is about telling a story. The patient buys the story and this brings about the desired change in him. So how do we tell a story? There are two ways that come immediately to mind.

The first way is to find out how the bio-computer was programmed in the first place to make you unhappy. When you know how, it is possible then to change the end of the story. As time changes and a person becomes more mature and responsible for themselves they hopefully learn to stop playing the 'Blame Game.' The circumstances in their lives change and it becomes necessary to change the way they react to situations. Unfortunately their bio-computers often make outdated pictures or people talk to themselves as if they were less mature or younger than they really are. If the images they make in the bio-computer don't apply any more then it is necessary to re-write the story so that the talking and/or pictures they make to think, become more appropriate. There are times in your life when traumas occur that will make certain pictures or dialogue more likely to lead to specific behaviour. For a fuller understanding of these conditions see my book 'How to Become the Parent you Never Had.' I will list here First, Second and Third line traumas with the conditions which each line causes. Knowing about the conditions caused by each line will help in making more appropriate stories.

First line traumas occur from conception to a few hours after birth. [See Arthur Janov's 'Imprints. The lifelong effects of the birth experience']. They are often life or death situations when the birthing baby experiences feelings of impending doom, with the resultant behaviour of depression, [they stop feeling, it's all they can do] or being scared stiff of dying, or if the pain becomes too great then to die becomes preferable. In later life the adult shows the behaviour of depression, or unreasonable fear of death. [It's got to happen eventually so there is no point in being afraid of it, thus condemning yourself to a living death and perpetual unhappiness]. If the pain level gets so great that the birthing baby would prefer to die, the grown adult may often seek that alternative as a way out of unpleasantness, even when there may be a much better way out. If these behaviours become stuck in adult life then it is necessary to change the end of the story. They did get out safely and it can never happen exactly the same again, and anyway it is all over now. [The difficult birth is over].

The organs affected with resultant conditions by first line trauma are listed below:

BLOOD VESSELS giving rise to Migraine or Arthritis
HEART—Palpitations, Angina, Heart Attack
CHEST—Asthma, Speech Difficulties
STOMACH—Ulcers
COLON—Spastic Colon

Difficulties with the cord at birth lead to:

Anorexia [See my book 'It's a Bit of a Mouthful']
Respiration Difficulties
Speech Difficulties
Choking Feelings

One way to test for cord trauma is to place a length of inch rubber tubing round the neck and vibrate it very quickly. Most people with cord trauma will make very bad images, inside their head, when you do that and will find it intolerable and react to it out of all proportion.

Too much early pain will result in almost total blocking out of reality thus leaving the child and later adult, insensitive to what is going on around them. They are too busy making negative birth images inside their head to notice anything else. This leads them to live in these negative pictures in their head and to be out of touch with their real needs and feelings and the needs and feelings of others.

First line traumas also lead to a host of other psychological difficulties listed below:

1. They learn what security is in the womb [see 'How to Become the Parent you Never Had'] but if the journey out is too difficult then they are obsessed with making negative images inside their head of how unsafe the world is, with the resultant fear that nowhere is secure. If you live in the world you might as well make it as pleasant a place as you can. There is nothing to be gained in hating it. [If you have to do something, don't hate it. See 'How not to use your mind' in the previous chapter].

2. Claustrophobia and the left over feelings of Agoraphobia [see 'How to Become the Parent you Never Had'] are also born out of the feelings learned at birth.

3. Feelings of unworthiness, or 'I am not fit to be here' [on this earth] come from the wipe-out feelings many people experience at birth. [If the birth is difficult the baby feels it is being got rid of, 'Wiped-out', shouldn't be here]. These feelings lead to the later adult having a feeling of lack of trust

in anyone, [they keep on making images inside their head of the wipe-out, so if mother and the world did that to me how can I trust anyone, or the world?]. They constantly experience excessive fears and panic attacks because of the internal images in their head that have nothing to do with reality, but with the birth experience. A treatment for these conditions is to rewrite the story and give it a happy ending thereby changing the images in the bio-computer.

4. If the new born baby is left to fend for itself immediately after birth, the later adult is all too often making visual or auditory images of the fear of being alone, inside their bio-computer. This leads to the 'psychological vampire,' the person who is over-dependent, will not make decisions for themselves [after all, the decision to come out of the womb hurt me therefore I will not trust my decisions]. Once again, a way to make changes in this person is to rewrite the story with a happy ending.

Second line traumas occur from a few hours after birth until about the age of six years old. These traumas occur because of the baby's inability to communicate fully its needs to the outside world, so they are really a cry for help. The young baby cannot satisfy its own needs at this tender age and has to have someone else do that for them. If these needs are neglected their behaviour becomes attention-seeking and leads to a new set of visual or auditory image-making in the bio-computer. [I will use the term visual or auditory image to mean seeing pictures of, or talking to self, thereby thinking which leads to feelings. [V->K. A->K.].

Unmet needs in a child from a few hours after birth to about six years of age may lead the later adult to make very negative images about emotions. They become non-affective, non-expressive with their feelings and emotions. They are afraid to show their emotions because of the horror images inside their bio-computer. If a child is not allowed to express all its feelings, both positive and negative, during this formative time they become emotionally blunted for the rest of their lives. This often results in defending against ones self interests and needs, or even denying they have needs. Or they become the opposite and are over-emotional and demanding. They use their behaviour without realizing it, to constantly gain attention, even when they are adults, and even when the attention is not the sort of recognition they want. They become the classic Freudian Hysteric with an excessive emotional dependency but no real focus for it to be directed towards.

This behaviour often reinforces the depressive moods learned at birth. That's why depression is often difficult to pin down to what started it off in the first place. [It was first learned at birth but reinforced later]. So second liners show a tendency towards wife bashing, child abusing including both physical trauma to the child and sexual abuse. [See next chapter].

Other behaviours that can be attributed to traumas that occurred in the formative years include illness phobias, cancer phobia, asthma, hair pulling, alopecia, nail bitting, thumb sucking, bed wetting, impotence, frigidity, skin conditions like acne, eczema, and rashes, blushing and even psoriasis. Psoriasis is always made worse when the person is upset or under stress.

A treatment for these conditions, like the first liners, is to rewrite the end of the story with a happier ending. As the patients are probably older they should be able to more easily fend for themselves and satisfy their own 'REAL' needs.

Third line traumas occur from about four years of age to the present day. There is an overlap of second and third line trauma because it depends on the child's ability to convey its needs to the adults round it at the time. It also depends on the adult's willingness to listen to the child and make sense out of what the child is saying, and be able to react appropriately to the child's needs. If the parent can't react appropriately, or the child can't communicate its needs, trauma occurs. This is when it becomes necessary, when helping the grown adult to make changes to enable, they themselves, to become the parent they never had. Unfortunately many parents cannot react appropriately because they are too busy inside with their own internal pictures to see the child's pictures, their truths are different so the parent abuses their child, often without knowing it, and in most cases with no intent of abuse. [See next chapter on Abuse]. These traumas occur between the patient and the world and the people in it. They lead to another set of behaviours different from first and second liners. Third liners are highly intellectualized individuals with less body control, less co-ordination, less sex drive or highly symbolized sexual activity. They tend to relate to ideas or numbers rather than being able to relate in an emotional way to other human beings. The man quoted in Chapter 3 who was unable to meet people face to face and who thought of the area between his eyes as a cassette player is a typical third liner. Third liners tend to show excessive fear of humiliation, arguments, and have extreme rivalry when it comes to their need for love and attention. They often suffer from reactive depression and psycho-sexual disorders. For examples of all these three trauma periods in our life see 'How to Become the Parent you Never Had'. A treatment for all three periods is to rewrite the stories, with a happier ending. [See the exercises in the above book and in 'It's a Bit of a Mouthful'].

2. Story telling by Metaphor to create change

Another way to tell a story to help someone to change is to tell a story in metaphor. When you do tell a metaphorical story, in order to understand what you are saying a person has to use their own senses and will make pictures, or talk to themselves about the things you are saying. When they are doing this it is impossible not to also use some of their own internal pictures to construct the new pictures about your metaphor. The programmes in their own bio-computer will be affected by the reconstruction of new pictures and internal talking as they try to understand your story. They will do this without being aware of the change so no resistance is encountered. This method therefore provides a very sophisticated and subtle way to change someone. I quoted a metaphor for change in my book 'It's a Bit of a Mouthful' in the last chapter. I would like you to look at it once again so I will repeat the metaphor part here and underline and bracket my comments in the text so that you may understand the desired result more clearly.

EXERCISE 2.   Metaphorical Story

'I would like you, for a moment, to think about your eyes. *[The eyes are visual and make pictures so in order to think about them you will make pictures].* They are your windows on to the world. You can send messages out from them. You can show love, hate, hunger, anger, fear, guilt and all your emotions, just by looking in different ways. *[It is hoped the patient will make pictures of looking differently at their problem].* At the same time your eyes can take messages in. When a light beam falls on to your eye the lens at the front of your eye concentrates the beam on to small cells, in the shape of rods and cones, at the back of your eye. These cells as a result of the light being concentrated on them produce certain chemicals. Those chemicals **excite the nerve at the back of your eye and create** *[It is hoped that the patient will become excited about creating new pictures].* an electrical impulse to pass back along the nerve through the hole in the back of your eyeball into the brain. And still you haven't seen anything. The nerve in the brain then crosses over to the other side of the brain and **excites more nerves.** *[As above].* And still you haven't seen anything. All this would happen if you were asleep and someone gently opened your eyelid and looked into your eye. If you didn't wake up you wouldn't see anything.

The nerves that have now been excited send an impulse to the visual centre in your brain to alert and wake up that part of your brain and at last you see something. *[It is hoped that your brain will wake up and see new ways out of your stuck state].* At the same time other nerves send impulses to your **memory centre to help you to identify whatever you are now seeing.** *[Your memory will help you identify what you want to change].* Your memory centre has millions of little circuits with all sorts of memories.

There was an interesting programme on the television sometime ago about a girl who was blind and the eye surgeons decided if they did an operation on her eyes **she may be able to see.** *[You may be able to see a change. The girl was blind and hopefully she will see, which is a change for her].* They did the operation and when the bandages were removed, much to **everyone's delight, she could see.** *[It will delight you to see something different].* They did some very interesting experiments while the girl was sitting at a table. They placed a cup on the table and asked her if she knew what it was. She didn't know what it was until they pushed it towards her and asked her to pick it up. When her hands touched it she laughed and said, 'It's a cup.' She had no visual memory of a cup because she had never seen a cup before, but she had a tactile memory of a cup because she had drunk out of a cup many times and touched a cup many times. *[Change from V-)K. all the time as this also produces a hypnotic state without a formal induction]* As soon as she touched it she recognised it as a cup. **She had to learn all over again what everything looked like before she could visually identify what everything was.** *[You can learn again to be unstuck in your behaviour by making new pictures. She did].*

All our memories are stored in little compartments in our brain. Those compartments could be like your bedroom with wardrobes and a chest of drawers and a dressing table and perhaps a bookshelf for your books. You have **specific places to keep all your special things.** *[You have specific senses to make all your special images].* Sometimes if your things have just been washed, or you have just been looking at them, and you haven't yet had time to put them away, you may need your bedroom, because guests are coming to visit you, and you want to put your guests' coats on your bed while they are with you. You may just push your things into the wardrobe to make the room look tidy for the time being, but after they have gone **you will have to go back and tidy up properly, and put all your things in their proper place.** *[Some of the pictures you are using are not in their right time. They are from some other time. You need to make some more pictures in their right time—NOW to tidy up your thoughts].*

One day you may be walking down the high street and while you are passing a little Boutique, there in the window on a model is the most beautiful outfit, **just your colour and style.** *[Colour and style are visual so make pictures about what suits you psychologically].* You can't believe your luck because it has been reduced from a ridiculous price to a **real bargain.** *[People can't resist a bargain especially if it suits them].* You can't resist going in and asking the sales person if you can **try it on.** *[Try some new pictures to help yourself].* She/he is pleased to help you and shows you to a changing room and brings the outfit. You quickly take off the clothes you are wearing and put on the new ones and you turn to look at yourself in the mirror. When you see the new outfit a thrill goes right through you. **It fits you perfectly. It does something for you, [V->K]** shows off all your best qualities. It's just your colour. *[Your new picture will help you look and feel better. When this exercise is over it is often useful to ask what colour the outfit was. The colour may give a clue to what is in the patient's unconscious mind at the time. Red is often angry, Blue is depression, Green is doubt, Yellow is fear, Black is without hope. Always check by asking the patient what they associate with the colour they mention as there are always exceptions and the person may not be responding to the metaphor in this part but to the memory of a particular outfit. That may be important too, so ask about it. If the outfit was associated with a pleasant memory you may want to use the memory later].* **It seems to bring out your best personality and makes you feel very confident.** *[Make pictures of what makes you confident].* You decide to have it, so you take it off and put on the clothes you came in with. Taking the new outfit to the sales person you say you will take it, so she/he wraps it up for you and you pay the money and go out of the shop.

Outside, you can't really believe everything you thought inside the shop, so you hurry home and rush up to your bedroom. There, you pull off the wrapping and *examine the outfit again. [See if your new images still seem better].* It still looks just as good and all the stitching is perfect and there are no marks on it. Quickly you once again take off your clothes and try on the new outfit. It looks even better, **fits you even better than you dared think. You feel a million dollars in it. You are very pleased with yourself.** *[It is always good to feel good and happy].*

You decide you don't want to wear it right now, but will

keep it for a special occasion, so you take it carefully off and once again put your old clothes back on. You go with it to your wardrobe to hang it up but when you open your wardrobe door you find all the hangers are in use. You don't have a spare one to hang your beautiful new outfit on so you have to look through all your things until you find an old one. **One that doesn't fit any more, that is worn, or out of fashion. One that does nothing for you, or that you have ceased to like. One that doesn't suit your new personality.** *[Change the old images to ones that suit you more as you are now].* When you find one that is no use to you anymore you take it out and place your new one on that hanger and put it carefully in your wardrobe and close the door. **You feel good, even just knowing it is there, when you want it.** *[You can feel good knowing you can change].* You take the old one and send it off to Oxfam, or cut it up for dusters, or just put it in the dustbin.

You feel very pleased with yourself. **It's always necessary, once in a while, to look through your old things and have a good clean out. You throw away the old useless things, which you have accumulated over the years, discarding those which do nothing for you anymore.** *[Every now and then you have to update all your programmes in your bio-computer to keep up with now].* Your mind is just like that.'

I have underlined most of the metaphors in the above story, there are a few more. It is unlikely that your unconscious mind will pick up all of these metaphors but if it picks up one or two, changes can be made without the person even knowing how.

3. Another way to bring about change is to Reframe for change

This process is described very fully in Bandler and Grinder's book 'Reframing'. Briefly, reframing has seven steps to the process.

EXERCISE 3.

[1]. It is necessary to identify what it is you need to change.

This is sometimes not always obvious because of defensive behaviour and secondary gains. The following question will sometimes help to recognise what is it that you need to change. 'What is it that you want to do, be, or feel that you can't do, be, or feel without my help?' Sometimes it is about stopping doing, being, or feeling that you want. When you have this answer you can move on to part two of the process.

[2]. Ask the part responsible for the unwanted behaviour when it is listening, paying attention and wanting to help, to gently lift a finger on one hand. [See ideo-motor finger response in previous books].

[3]. When a finger lifts, congratulate the part for wanting to help, but remind it that the way it is helping has become the problem. All behaviour is an attempt to help a person, often to solve a problem, but frequently the way the bio-computer is helping someone to do something becomes the problem, either because there is a better way, or because the present way is no longer relevant. In any case if you want to change a behaviour it is because the present behaviour is making the person unhappy. There is always more than one way to do anything and perhaps another way would result in more happiness. If it doesn't you can always go back to the old way. Ask the part lifting the ideo motor finger if it is willing to consider another way to help. If so lift the finger again.

[4]. When the finger lifts, then ask the patient to contact another part of the mind. A part we shall call the creative part of the mind. This part is responsible for all the pros and cons of behaviour. When that part is listening, paying attention and wanting to help it could lift another finger on the other hand. [Opposite hand to step 2].

[5]. Now ask both parts to get together in the unconscious mind to discuss and debate better ways of achieving the desired goal. When they have found at least three better ways of achieving the goal let both fingers and hands come together as a sign of agreement and acceptance of the better ways to behave.

[6]. When the fingers and hands come together ask the rest of the mind to check that there are no parts that object to this new unconscious behaviour. If none object, let a finger rise

to indicate agreement in the whole of the mind.

[7]. Now do a 'future pace.' [See Glossary for 'future pace']. Ask the patient to imagine they have achieved a new way to behave and ask them how they feel about being able to do, be, or feel about the answer to part 1. Their face should show pleasure if what you have done has worked. If it doesn't you have missed something out. This reframe should leave the patient with a better self image and a greater feeling of happiness and therefore it should show externally on the patient's face.

For the above technique to work you don't need to know what the alternative behaviour is, as you are asking the unconscious mind to find a number of alternatives which you can try out until you find one that makes you more comfortable and happy. If the first ones don't achieve that, do another reframe until it does work. These techniques are described more fully in both my previous books and in Bandler and Grinder's book 'Reframing'.

4. Creating new anchors and collapsing old as a method of change

There are various situations in which a person is used to doing a particular behaviour which may or may not have anything to do with that behaviour. For instance a smoker may always have a cigarette with his morning cup of coffee. I don't smoke so I never think of having a cigarette with my morning coffee, but someone who does smoke may find that they can't enjoy their coffee without a cigarette. The coffee is an anchor that makes them have to have a cigarette. Anchors like the one described above are very easily established and play a large part in creating stuck behaviours. 'Stuck behaviours' are often, but not always, behaviours which we would rather not have, but we seem unable to do anything about. Anchors can, of course, be both positive or negative. It's impossible to go through life without creating hundreds of them. For instance those of us who are lucky enough to share a bed with a delightful partner find we always sleep on our own side of the bed. Have you ever tried to sleep on the wrong side of the bed? Your partner's side. Most people would find they wouldn't sleep very well if they did. My wife and I, when we are travelling and have single beds, still sleep on the same sides even when we are not in the same bed. If we don't, we don't sleep nearly as well. Some people play the 'Me Tarzan, you Jane' game. The man always sleeps nearest the door to protect the woman. This is just another example of an anchor, this one doesn't really affect a person positively or negatively as it doesn't matter which side they sleep so long as it is the usual side.

The marathon which we all ran to be here is an example of a positive anchor which is useful to have and is quoted in Chapter 2, exercise one. It is always useful to feel we asked to be here, and we have as much right to be here as anyone else, etc.

When we are helping someone to make changes in their behaviour it is very useful to look at the anchors surrounding that behaviour, and see if any of those which result in being stuck with the unwanted behaviour, can be changed. It is quite a simple procedure to collapse unwanted anchors or build new wanted ones.

I was attending an N.L.P. workshop early this year and as part of the workshop, about mid-afternoon on the second day, we were asked to split up into small groups to practice creating anchors. I was with a group of friends from Scotland and one of my friends was having some difficulty with his breathing. I asked him what the trouble was and he said 'It's these damn nylon carpets. When I came into the hotel last night I noticed all the carpets were synthetic. I had to go straight out to my car and get some of my inhalers. I am allergic to nylon, it gives me asthma. It was bad all night, I had to use my inhalers four or five times during the night. And it's been bad all day.' We could see that, he was still having difficulty in breathing that afternoon and his face was a little blue. He went on to say, 'Actually I can't wait to get home, all our carpets there are pure wool and my breathing is excellent when I am at home.' Without realizing it he had just told me how to make his breathing easier.

I asked him to tell me again exactly what he had been thinking when he first noticed that the carpets were nylon.

He began to tell me and very quickly, as he was telling me, his breathing got even worse. As it was getting worse he was looking upwards and obviously was picturing the nylon carpets all over again. He was making internal pictures of the carpets and at the same time feeling he couldn't breathe. He was programming his bio-computer to make his breathing bad and his mind did just that to him. It was working perfectly, he had just told it the wrong thing to do. When his breathing was at its worst I gently squeezed his right shoulder and in doing so I created a negative anchor to squeezing his right shoulder. That was all I needed to do to create this anchor. This meant that the next time I squeezed his right shoulder, in exactly the same place as I had squeezed it to set up the anchor, his breathing would be bad again. He then went on to tell me that he said to himself, 'I had better go and get my inhalers or I won't be able to breathe.' I asked him what telling himself that he had better go out to the car and get his inhaler or he wouldn't be able to breathe was programming his mind to do. He looked a little surprised as he realized he had programmed himself not to breathe easily. He said, 'Do you really mean I did that to myself without knowing?'

I said, **'It looks that way.'** As I said that his breathing got much easier so I squeezed his right shoulder and it got worse again. I had fired the anchor that I had created earlier and his breathing got worse. He looked upwards, as it was getting worse, so firing the anchor had made him make those pictures of nylon carpets that makes his breathing bad.

He looked at me with amazement on his face and said, 'How did you do that?'

I said, **'I just fired the anchor I made when you were telling me about the nylon carpets. You do that all the time when you see nylon carpets. Nylon carpets are your anchor for not being able to breathe easily, just as my squeezing your shoulder was my anchor to stop you breathing easily.'**

I then asked him to tell me how his carpets at home help his breathing.

He said, 'Well when I found I was allergic to Nylon we made sure all our carpets in the house were all wool and had no synthetic material in them at all.' As he was telling me this, he was looking upwards and his breathing became calmer than it had been all the time he had been with us. The blue tinge left his face and it became a nice pale pink. It had been slightly cyanosed [bluish due to the lack of oxygen] all the time, before I asked him to tell me about his carpets at home.

At the moment his breathing and colour in his face began to improve, I squeezed his left shoulder, and in doing so I created an anchor to breathe easily. I now had a positive anchor in his left shoulder and a negative anchor in his right shoulder. Squeezing his left shoulder would help him to breathe, while squeezing his right shoulder would make his breathing laboured. I wanted to stop nylon carpets from making his breathing difficult.

I asked him to tell me again about nylon carpets. As he did so his breathing began to get bad again and the pink colour began to drain from his face, but this time, just as this was happening I squeezed both shoulders at exactly the same time. You cannot have both good and bad breathing at the same time, just as you can't picture nylon carpets and all wool carpets at the same time. The timing for both creating anchors and collapsing them is very important. You have to do both these two things just as the feelings are rising to their peak, before or after the peak doesn't work. If you want to work with anchors, it is important that you first practice creating them with a trainer, otherwise you will get it wrong most of the time. As I squeezed both his shoulders at the same time, his breathing became normal and the colour in his face improved. I had collapsed both anchors on his shoulders, neither of them would work again unless they were set up again. At the same time, however, because he was thinking about nylon carpets I had also collapsed his anchor to having difficulty with his breathing, when he saw or thought about nylon carpets. They would not trigger off difficulty in breathing any more, unless you set them up again. His breathing remained O.K. for the rest of the day in spite of the nylon carpets.

You can collapse anchors as easily as that when you see all the external signs in the patient. Remember you should always be able to see external signs of what is going on inside the bio-computer. If you can't then it probably hasn't worked. I hope by now you can see how important it is to observe very closely a person with whom you hope to make changes. I also helped my friend to create another anchor which he could use for himself if ever his breathing became laboured again. I asked him to think once more about breathing at home and when he felt his breathing getting really good he was to rub the tip of his thumb over the tips of his other fingers on the same hand. He did this, thereby creating an anchor to help him to breathe by rubbing his thumb over his fingers. Any time he had any difficulty in breathing all he was to do to collapse the negative anchor was to rub his thumb over his fingers.

I met him about six months later and he said he had been worlds better. He hadn't had any attacks of asthma and now and then if his breathing became a little difficult, he had done his trick with his thumb and his breathing became easy again. He kept reinforcing his positive anchor with his thumb, in the same way as I had taught him to do it in the first place. I like to think it is a good thing to have resources and control, at your fingertips.

I have used both creating new and positive anchors, as well as collapsing negative anchors, in many patients with a wide range of stuck states, with equal success. If, however, that doesn't work then do something else. Remember you should be able to see it working on the outside, if it's going to work internally in the bio-computer, but nothing works for everybody.

A very useful time to collapse anchors is when someone wants to stop doing something, which quite a large part of them wants to continue doing. Take smokers, for example. Most smokers who want to stop smoking have a part that enjoys smoking and doesn't really want to stop. If that part is larger than the part which wants to give it up, you have a battle on your hands which you most probably will not win, unless you first do something about the part that enjoys smoking. To do this you can set up an anchor, in the same way as I described by squeezing a shoulder, for the enjoyment experienced when smoking, while they are thinking about smoking. Then ask them to think about something that they are sure they would never do under any circumstances. Something that they feel very good about not wanting to do and when they are in that programme, anchor that on the other shoulder. When both anchors are firmly fixed and tested by firing both separately and noting the result, you can then ask the person to think about the enjoyment he gets when smoking and at the height of the person's experience, fire both anchors. You should be able to see the pleasure disappear from their face as you fire both anchors. The part which enjoyed smoking before should then be able to take it, or leave it, when it comes to smoking.

5. Spiegel's Split Screen as a method for change

Most of the techniques being described below require the patient to visualize. If they have difficulty in visualizing in their conscious mind you can either teach them to visualize consciously as described earlier in this book [Chapter 1]. Or you can explain that to think everyone has to use all their senses but some people visualize in their unconscious mind as a transparency and then consciously think about it as an abstract thought. Ask them to do the tests for visualization described in Chapter 1 until they accept that they do visualize on one level of thinking. If they still have difficulty, ask them just to think about the images you are asking them to make, as a thought or concept. When they do that they will be making transparency pictures in their unconscious mind to think about the images. It doesn't matter whether they do it on a conscious or unconscious level.

EXERCISE 4.

A much easier way to reframe behaviour and change it, is to use Spiegel's Split screen technique. For this approach you need to know what you want to change and what you would like in its place. When you know both these things it is simple to make it work. You ask the patient to close their eyes and make an image of a screen split down the middle, or it could be two screens, in front of them. The screens should at first be near to them. On one of the screens place the behaviour you don't want to have, and see or feel it going away from you, far away to the other side of the room. While that behaviour is far away on the other side of the room, place the behaviour you want to have on the other screen and bring only that half of the screen back close to you, leaving the behaviour you don't want, far away on the other side of the room. Imagine what it would be like to have the behaviour you want, then open your eyes and be that person with that behaviour. Repeat this exercise, taking only about ten to twenty seconds to do it each time, every two to three hours until your behaviour is the one you want. Notice you are giving to your bio-computer a direction for your behaviour to go. The old unwanted one away and the new wanted behaviour towards you.

The boxer I was telling you about at the end of the last chapter had an image of himself freezing in the ring in the first screen which he then pushed away from himself. In the other half, or the second screen he saw himself as a living, boxing machine, getting on with the job of boxing and finishing his opponent off as soon as the occasion presented itself, or even making that occasion happen so that he could finish him off. He won his next fight very convincingly and has won every fight since. [See later in this chapter the slide change for his championship fight].

6. Double mirror technique for change

The double mirror technique is a variation of the split screen technique which I thought I had invented, but later I read about it in one of Richard Bandler's books. I had not read about it before I started using this technique, so for me I had invented it. It just goes to show if an idea is good you are not going to be the only one to think of it. As with the split screen above you need to know what programme you want to change and what you want in its place, for the two mirror technique.

You also want the person to be able to visualize, but this

can be unconsciously as a transparency as described above. If they can't visualize consciously just tell them to think about what you are saying as a thought.

EXERCISE 5.

The technique is to tell them to close their eyes and imagine that they are standing between two full length mirrors. One in front of them and one behind them. They are to look at the mirror behind them first and see a reflection of themselves with the behaviour which they want to change. See the reflection fade and become colourless, shades of grey and get smaller and fainter and in your mind walk away from it.

Then turn to look at the mirror in front of you. In this mirror, imagine yourself with the behaviour you would like to have. See this reflection brighter, clearer, more colourful, bigger and walk towards it. As you do, see how much more you like yourself in this mirror with the new behaviour.

If the person doing this exercise is smiling, you know it's working. If they are not showing an increased pleasure somehow on their face, you know it's not working. They will always show externally what they are feeling on the inside. If they are not feeling it on the inside it's not working. You will have to find another way to make them see and feel [V->K] that to change would be pleasurable and then when you see it in their face you know it is working. When you can see the pleasure in their face point it out to them by saying 'see how much happier you are doing- [the new behaviour]'. Their smile should broaden. When it does, ask them to step right into, and through, the mirror in front of them, then open their eyes.

I have used this technique many times with all sorts of behaviour. Recently I had great success with a stammerer who I also added auditory images in the mirror. In the mirror behind him as well as seeing himself unhappy and avoiding communication and contact with other people, he also heard himself stammering badly. I had him make this image fade and go away, and then in the mirror in front of him he was to see himself much happier, going towards people, looking forward to meeting with them and communicating with them and at the same time to hear himself talking without any difficulty. [V->K and A->K]. When I asked him to do this he had a great smile on his face, obviously enjoying it, so I knew it had worked. His bio-computer was now program-med. I told him to do it five times a day for only twenty seconds at a time until he was talking well. He reported he hadn't had to do it at all, after he left my rooms, as he was talking well as soon as he left. It is often a good idea to include an auditory image as well as a visual one when you are changing people.

I was working with a lady today who was very unhappy and depressed and suicidal. She keeps on making pictures of how she hated herself as a child which makes her feel she hates herself now. I took some time to find out what she was doing to feel so bad. She said she was afraid of letting go, going out of control. I explained she was already out of control. She was letting her mind drive her at random and it was making a lot of pictures which had nothing to do with now but to do with her childhood. As she was no longer a child then to let her mind regress to childish pictures was already out of control. Would she like me to teach her how to stop being out of control?

She said, 'That would be nice.' I asked her to pretend she was totally in control and shut her eyes to picture how she would look when that was the case, and to nod her head when she could picture that. After only about 30 seconds she nodded her head. **'Good! now see yourself in the picture, getting brighter and closer, and have some friends with you and hear laughter.'** I knew she saw and heard it because you could see it on her face. It was the first time I had seen her smile in three visits to my consulting rooms. I asked her to open her eyes and tell me about the picture she had just seen. She smiled again as she told me about being dressed in red and laughing and joking with her friends who accepted her easily. I knew by this that normally she must have some difficulty in being comfortable with her friends.

While she was telling me this I noticed she was rubbing her fingers with her thumb and I looked at her thumb and said, **'Be your thumb what is it saying to the rest of you?'**

She said, 'I do that to comfort myself.'

'No,' I said, 'I don't want to know what you do, I can see that, I want to know what your thumb is thinking about the rest of you?'

'It's saying get going. Get on with it'

'Excellent, Let's do that shall we?'

'Yes please!'

'Close your eyes and imagine you are standing between two large full length mirrors, one in front of you and one behind you. Turn to look into the mirror behind you. In that mirror see an image of yourself dressed in dull clothing. See the whole reflection grey, dull, lonely, quiet and frightening, getting smaller and push that reflection away by walking away from the mirror. Now turn round and see a picture of yourself dressed in red in the mirror in front of you. See yourself among your friends laughing and joking. As you walk up to the mirror see yourself happy, laughing, getting bigger, brighter, more in control than you have ever been because you are driving your mind. See how your thumb is telling you to get on with it' [Her thumb had already started to rub her fingers, I was just pointing it out, and reminding her what it was telling her]. I could see it was working as she had a big smile all over her face. **'Now step right up and into the mirror in front of you.'**

'Oh yes' she said.

'Now open your eyes'

She opened them still smiling and said, 'That feels much better, I know where I am going now.'

'Now do that again, six times but open your eyes after each time you step into the mirror in front of you.' She did it six times.

'How do you find doing that?'

'It is easier to see the mirror in front of me.'

'If you try to look at the mirror behind you what happens?'

'The one in front comes up.' **'Does it do that automatically?'**

'Yes.'

'Good!'

It is important that you tell the person to open their eyes every time they have stepped into the mirror in front of them, as this then ends the programme. If you don't open your eyes and go back to the mirror behind you without opening the eyes you are just going backwards and forwards in the same programme. You want to leave no doubt which way you want your mind to take you. Notice the way this technique is giving a direction for the mind to go. Leave the old behaviour behind you. See it get smaller- a possible time regression- you learned it when you were smaller. Move ahead to the new behaviour making it bigger is reversing the time regression suggesting growing out of it. Seeing it making you happier is very important as this is what makes it work. The mind will always try to help you if you show it how, convincingly enough.

7. Zoom slide for change

Again this is a very similar technique to the two mirror technique described above. It is always necessary when using techniques to change someone, that you check up on how that person's bio-computer works, because there are variations in the way people work their brains. Let us look again at how people think and make feelings. Most people do V->K. or A->K. to think or feel. They make a picture then feel it, or they hear a sound, possibly talk to themselves, then they feel that. If you are working with someone who wants to change, you should ask them what the behaviour they wish to change, makes them feel. It generally is a negative feeling. It may be something which they would like to feel better about. These techniques not only help people to change experiences that they are not happy about, but it also makes some behaviours even more enjoyable than they already are. For instance someone may find sex O.K. but they could really take it or leave it. They may feel that being like that about sex is missing out and would much rather find sex very enjoyable. It is possible to help someone do something like that when you know how their bio-computer works.

These techniques are about looking at how people think,

and then using that to teach them to think differently and therefore feel different. Remember, Descartes said the only truth in the mental processes is 'I think therefore I am.' If we can make them think differently then they are different.

As Kierkegaard said, 'Whenever we translate experience into words or thoughts there is a distortion of that experience.' Richard Bandler says words and thoughts are only inadequate labels for those experiences. Richard Bandler also said the order of sequence of experience, like words in a sentence, affects their meaning. For example if you have a bad experience you have made some negative images in your bio-computer. If you then have another experience that in some way is similar to or representative of the first, you are very likely to make the second experience negative, because of the negative images made by the first experience. That is the case even when there is nothing negative in the second experience that any outsider could see. An outsider hasn't got your internal images to think and feel by, so they see your behaviour as irrational, or a distortion of THE TRUTH. [Really it is a distortion of their truth]. There is no absolute truth, the truth is only as you see it. And your truth is affected by all your past experiences, as is theirs. Unfortunately this difference in truths, which is governed by each person's internal pictures which are always different and personal to everybody, leads to one person abusing another, more often than not, with no intention of abuse, or without realizing it. [See next Chapter, on Abuse].

Unfortunately most people are prisoners of their own thoughts and stuck with their behaviour because they haven't given their bio-computer any direction in which to take them. They just let their brain take them randomly in all directions, or worse still, let other people run them for them. They do this by taking images from their past experiences which may well have, in real terms, very little to do with the current experience.

The purpose of life itself is to become responsible for yourself. [See my book 'How to Become the Parent you Never Had']. You must become responsible for how you think and feel and when you do you can be any damn thing you want to be. What you want to be must be better than what you are, in your thoughts, for any of these techniques to work. It's no good someone else wanting you to be better, you have to think and feel that to change would be better for you personally.

So when we have someone who genuinely thinks and feels it would be better to change let us look at how they feel bad.

EXERCISE 6.

Think of something you want to change in your life that makes you feel bad. Think of the last time you did it or felt it strongly. How did you do that? How did you think of it, or feel it, or remember it? You can only have used one or more of your five senses to do that. That's the only way you can think. You either saw something, or you heard something, often yourself talking to yourself, or you smelt something, or you tasted something, then you felt something. You may think you just felt something without any of the first senses being used, but if you persevere ninety nine times out of a hundred you will first see or hear something before you feel. When you know what you saw or heard then try altering all of the variants in Chapter 1, one at a time and see which makes the biggest changes in the feelings connected to your memory.

If you first saw a picture about your memory where do you see it now? Is it close to you? How big is it? How bright is it? Is it coloured? Try to see if making it smaller makes the feelings worse or better. Does making it bigger make it worse or less unpleasant? Make the picture far away then close to, and see what effect that has on the memory. Make it clear then out of focus and see what effect that has. Try all the visual variants and notice which have the greatest effect on the memory, which ones make the feeling about the memory worse and which ones make the feelings better. When you know, be sure to remember which variants make the feelings worse and which better.

EXERCISE 7.

Now do the same about a good memory that makes you feel

good. Find out which variants make the good feelings, about the memory, stronger and weaker.

EXERCISE 8.
If you first heard something about the bad memory that made you feel bad, try altering the auditory variants listed in Chapter 1 and note which variants make the feeling worse and which make it less bad. Make a note of these.

EXERCISE 9.
Now think of a good memory which starts with saying something good to yourself, and try the auditory variants and note which make the feeling stronger and which make the feeling weaker.

When you have all this information you are in a good position to make some good changes in a person's life. People always think about experiences by using their sensory systems, it's impossible for them to think without using the senses.

Now let us look the Zoom slide technique.

EXERCISE 10.   The Zoom Slide
To do the zoom slide ask the patient to imagine they have a slide or film projector. [It can be a still slide, or moving film depending on that person's own internal preferences. If a moving picture has a stronger effect, use a moving film, but if the patient making the change, finds a still picture makes the feelings stronger, then use a still slide]. Tell them the projector is specially fitted with a zoom lens that can zoom the picture away and make the picture small and far away, or bring it back to appear large and close. Make sure they understand this principle before you go on with this technique.

The first slide they are to look at is a slide of a film taken by themselves. They have the camera, so they are not in the film but everything else is in the film. This makes them dissociate from the first picture. The film in the camera is in black and white so the picture is in shades of grey, not coloured. The focus is also slightly out, so the picture isn't so clear. The picture is of what makes them feel bad and what they want to change, in their life. Not their whole life style but one aspect at a time. Have them see this picture, then zoom it away into the distance all the time getting smaller until they can hardly see it.

Then in part of the picture which is now small and far away they are to notice a small blur which they didn't notice before. Ask them to bring the picture back but as they do so, the blur is to grow bigger and clearer and take over the whole picture. The new picture has been taken by someone else so they [the person making the change in their life] are now in the film, and fully associated with it. The new picture, from the blur, is in full colour and with sharp focus so that everything is very clear. Now make it bigger and clearer and see that this new picture is about the change you would like to make in your life. This new picture fills the whole scene and completely replaces the old one.

When they have done that ask them to open their eyes to end this programme. Ask them how they found that. If it was O.K. and they found it easy, then ask them to repeat this exercise immediately. Tell them to do the exercise again, five times over, but each time open their eyes before doing it again, in order to end the programme with the good image each time. Never go back to the unwanted image without opening their eyes otherwise they are just making their mind go backwards and forwards and giving no clear direction to go. Tell them to do this as fast as they can. If they are taking more than ten seconds to do this, encourage them to do it faster. When they have done this five times, ask them if they found anything interesting in either of the pictures they were looking at. If it has worked they should find it gets harder to make the first picture, because the second picture keeps on coming in faster and faster. If this is found to be so test the change by asking them to make only the first picture and, once again, if it has worked the second picture will take over the first automatically. They shouldn't be able to see the first before the second one takes over. It has to be automatic if it is going to work. It is no good if they have to make it take over.

If it's automatic, every time they are triggered unconsciously to make the first picture the second one will automatically come in and they will think differently and be different. That's the whole essence of change. If it isn't absolutely automatic but nearly, do it some more times until it is. If it is nowhere near automatic you have either missed something out, or you have constructed the wrong pictures, or you should try something else.

Let us look at an actual case now of the lady in Chapter 1 who shook every time she had to demonstrate a product or be in front of people, who was always afraid she would dry up on 'stage'. I called her Carol. If you remember, she thought she had two people inside her. One large shaking mass of jelly and one little demon who made her get on with whatever she had to do.

The first picture Carol looked at, in black and white, was this large mass of shaking jelly next to the little demon who was trying to push her on stage. Carol wasn't in the picture herself, only the jelly and the demon. She was asked to zoom this picture far away and see the shaking jelly getting much smaller. The picture from the blur was in bright colour and we changed the little demon to a life size fairy godmother with a kind, encouraging face standing right next to Carol, so she was in this picture. The shaking jelly was only a tiny little piece, overshadowed by, and at the foot of, the fairy godmother. After Carol had zoomed these pictures five times, when I asked her if she had noticed anything interesting she said 'Yes the last time I did it the fairy godmother stamped on the jelly until it didn't exist any more.'

People will often add their own bit to the picture and make it work better.

I also did an auditory zoom with Carol, I am not sure if it was necessary after the first exercise, but I always feel it is better to overdo things, rather than under doing them. In the auditory zoom I had Carol hear herself saying 'You might dry up'. Then hear her fairy godmother say to her 'Of course you won't, you know all the product, and if you forget I will remind you.' The second time she repeated the auditory zoom Carol was to leave a word out of the first part but say all of the second part. The next time she left another word out of the first part and so on until there were no words left in the first part, so in the end she only said the last part of the auditory zoom. Carol also did a second auditory Zoom with the first part the same as above and the second half saying to her self I have as much right as anyone else to be here. [We did the marathon described in Exercise 1].

Then I asked Carol how she would think of herself when she was in control of her mind [see Chapter 1 pages 13 to 15]. She would see herself very differently when she was in control, so I asked her to make a picture of being in the driving seat of her mind. She again smiled and obviously enjoyed the picture. I also asked her to make a picture of trying to drive her mind from the back seat. The zoom, was to see in the first picture, a view from the back seat of the car, through her eyes, being driven at random to where she didn't want to be. Then to zoom that picture away and bring back the picture of herself in the front seat driving her mind everywhere she wanted to go. She did this zoom 5 times and looked really pleased with herself afterwards.

8. The Slide Change
Richard Bandler calls this technique the 'Swish' and he describes it excellently in his book 'Using your brain -for a Change.' I have used it extensively, to make agreeable and pleasant changes in people's behaviour for a wide range of complaints. The technique is as follows.

EXERCISE 11. The Slide Change [Richard Bandler's 'Swish']
The concept, for the person wishing to use this technique to make changes in their behaviour, is of a slide projector with a change bar. This bar is of the type that you can put two slides in it at the same time. One in the left of the projector and one in the right. If you push the left side of the bar into the projector you get one slide and to change the slide all you have to do is push in the right side and the picture changes instantly. It is necessary to make sure the patient understands this concept before you go any further.

The first imagined slide is taken by the patient themselves

with a black and white film so they are not in the picture. It can be slightly out of focus. The slide may be a still picture or a moving film. I will quote examples of both. The second imagined slide is taken by someone else so that the patient can see themselves in the film. It is in full colour and sharp focus. The first film can be a distance shot and the second film a close up.

The first imagined picture is of the situation where the behaviour occurs which the patient wishes to change. As soon as this picture is recognised, the patient is immediately asked to change it for the second imagined picture, which is a full colour film of the behaviour which they would rather have in place of the old behaviour which they wish to change. The change over from the first picture to the second has to be very quick, or as Richard Bandler says, in the time it takes to say the word, 'Swish'.

The patient is asked to close their eyes and picture in their mind the first picture, then very quickly to change the picture to the second one, in no more time than it takes to say, 'Swish.' After they have done that, they must open their eyes. Never go back to the first picture before you end and come out of the programme, by opening your eyes. Then repeat this exercise for about six times, opening your eyes each time before you make the first picture again. If you keep your eyes shut between making each exercise you are just going backwards and forwards in the same programme. You have to give your mind a direction to go in, from the first picture to the second. The slide change can be visual, or auditory, or both.

At the end of the sixth time, the patient should find it much harder to make the first picture and if they try to make only the first picture, the second should automatically come into their minds if the slide change has worked. If it hasn't, you either have made the wrong pictures, or you have left something out, or the second behaviour isn't that much more desired over the one which you wish to change. It is the patient's desire to make the change that makes it all work.

Now let us look at some actual cases in which we used the slide change, or 'swish', to create changes. I was working on a weekend course talking about oral gratification and demonstrating techniques to help a person to make changes in their behaviour. I asked if there was anyone among the audience who had a behaviour, in which the mouth played a part, which they felt they would like to change, but felt stuck with that behaviour. A charming young professional man volunteered and came and sat in the demonstration chair. He showed his hands and said, 'I would really like to stop biting my nails.'

His finger nails were all bitten very short and he quickly withdrew them showing he was embarrassed by anyone looking at them. I asked him to just pretend he had stopped biting his nails and then asked him to tell me how much he would like himself now that he no longer bit his nails. At first he struggled then he said, 'Well I would not have to hide my nails any more.'

I said, **'No I don't want something you would not have to do, I want something more positive than that.'**

'Well I would feel much more in control, and I would respect myself much more.'

'That's much better! Would you make a picture in your mind of this 'you' that you would respect much more, the 'you' more in control, and see how that looks.' He smiled and nodded, so I knew he saw a better self. I then asked him to give this picture of himself a sparkle and make it brighter and more colourful. He nodded again and said, 'That looks good.'

I asked him, **'What was the first thing he noticed about himself when he was about to bite his nails.'**

He said, 'I suppose it is the piece of nail in my mouth.'

I said, **'No before that, before you have actually bitten your nail.'** Once he has bitten his nail it's too late to stop him, he is actually in the programme.

He said, 'It's something to do with my hands, when I'm bored.' **'Good! now we can work and help you to make that change.'**

I explained the concept about the two slide projector and he agreed he understood that sort of projector. His first slide was a picture in black and white of a place where he may be bored and he was to see, as if out of his own eyes, his hand coming up towards his mouth to be bitten. It was not to reach his mouth because before it did he was to change the slide to a full colour picture, which someone else had taken of him. This second slide was a slide of the new person, who was totally in control, who liked himself much more, who had a sparkle about him, and would always find better ways of relieving boredom than lifting his hand to his mouth to bite his nails. Notice I didn't ask him to have a picture of himself with nice grown nails, because it would take a little time for them to grow. The picture was of him in control, with no desire to lift his hand and bite the nails. The second picture has to be possible fairly soon, so it has to be a process to achieve the desired end, if that end will take some time to be achieved, like dieting. It's no good picturing themselves at their target weight if that is going to take some time to achieve, so make a picture of a process which will in the end result in achieving the target weight.

I then told him to close his eyes and make the first picture and as soon as he saw his hand coming up to his mouth to quickly change the picture to the next slide and see himself with his hands nowhere near his mouth, then as soon as he had done this to open his eyes. He did that, so I told him to do it again a little quicker. He did it much quicker this time. I then told him to do that five times, opening his eyes after each time he made the second picture. I counted the five times for him as he did it because I wanted to let him give his full concentration on making the two changing pictures. I found through experience it is better to count for the patient as they do the exercise as they sometimes concentrate too hard on remembering how many times they were doing it, and not enough on actually doing the 'swish'. After he had done it five times, I asked him to just make the first picture and see what happens. He said, 'The second picture comes in automatically.' That's what we needed to know.

I then discussed the concept of him driving his mind, as opposed to his mind driving him to where he didn't want to go. [In his case to biting his nails]. We did a slide change of him in the back seat of his mind being driven to raise his hand to bite the nails. Then the change slide of him in the front seat of his mind in full control with a sparkle in his life. That too became automatic after five times.

A discussion followed involving the audience and someone asked how did my volunteer know he wouldn't bite his nails any more. He said. 'I don't know but my hands feel much more comfortable on my knees now, and I don't feel I want to lift them anywhere near my mouth, which I would have done before doing these exercises.'

I used a slide change with the lady I mention in Chapter 3, who found a letter in her husband's suit pocket from a mistress when she was taking his suit to the cleaners. The lady I was helping kept on seeing that letter in her mind over and over again. Doing that when the affair was over wasn't helping them to get on with each other, it just hurt her. She said she wished she could get it out of her mind. She said she would feel a much better person when she stopped punishing herself by reminding herself of that letter. So we did a slide change of the letter.

In the first slide she was to imagine she had taken a black and white picture, out of focus, of the letter in her hands and she was to imagine she could see that picture now. Before she was able to feel anything about this picture she was quickly to change that picture for a picture which someone else had taken, in full colour, with very clear focus of her husband and herself. In this second picture both her husband and herself were clearly, loving each other, very fondly. She was to close her eyes and see the first picture just appearing but very quickly change that picture for the second one in which her husband and herself were clearly in love. Then she had to open her eyes. I asked her to do this five times, opening her eyes after each time she made the second picture in her mind. After she had done that I asked her to make the picture of the letter again and see what happened. She reported the picture of her husband and her in love kept coming in every time she tried to make the picture of the letter.

We did the same sort of thing with the other lady I mention in Chapter 3, who kept seeing her husband in bed with his ex. mistress.

I also did a slide change with the commonwealth boxing champion who I helped to get over his difficulty in 'freezing' when he was boxing in the ring. Just before Glen won the championship he came for a 'top up' to help him with this important fight. In the first slide he imagined he saw his opponent looking menacingly at him. Quickly he changed this slide to one showing both Glen and his opponent, with Glen looking the much more menacing one and winning the commonwealth championship. After he had done this five times, opening his eyes after each time, I asked him how he felt. He said the room looked brighter. It did because he felt he was going to win. He won the championship the next night.

The skill in all these techniques is to help the patient to make the correct pictures for change and not leave anything out of the pictures.

I will describe the techniques for changing phobias in the chapter on phobias. [Chapter 7].

CHAPTER 5

Human abuse
How does one human being manage to abuse another so easily?

Have you ever thought how easy it is for practically everybody in the human race to abuse another person or persons, or even themselves, very often without even being aware of doing so? Sometimes they may be aware that their behaviour is hurting someone else, but rarely are they conscious of the enormous lasting damage it may have on that person and they may not even know why they are deliberately hurting someone else. Often the abuse becomes a compulsion over which the abuser seems to have no control.

Children have an enormous ability to hurt each other, often finding tremendous amusement in the infliction and with very little awareness of the devastating effect it may be having on the recipient. How do they do that and what can you do to help the abused?

Pete was the recipient of just such a cruelty. He is a seventeen year old who has opted out of the sixth form, no job to go to, no future, no girl friend, no nothing. As he sat down in my consulting room, for his first visit, I noticed how uncomfortable he looked. When I asked him what he hoped I could help him to do, be, or feel, that he couldn't do be or feel without my help, he became totally embarrassed. He fidgeted, squirmed and took about two and a half minutes to be able to say anything. Two and a half minutes of silence

73

seems like a very long time to wait for an answer but if your patient is obviously going through an ordeal inside his head and showing it on the outside, it's better to say nothing until he is ready and talking. If you interrupt him you may give him a defence to not tell you what is really hurting.

When he was ready he said, 'I smell!'

I looked at him and said, **'You say you smell.'** Notice I didn't say, **'You smell?,'** because he might have interpreted that as my saying he *did* smell, and at that time I didn't know if he did smell, or even what he smelt. Once again a painful silence.

'Yes I smell, my best friend told me I do. I know I do because whenever I went to school people would whisper and laugh and then run away. Or they might just sniff loudly and laugh. They seemed to be waiting to get away from me, or touching their noses and laughing.'

It was their laughing that told me somebody was having a good joke on him, but he was too involved in the pain to see that. **'What do you think you smell of?'** Notice, at this stage I'm not invalidating his belief that he smells. It's too early to do that, I haven't got enough from him to help him yet. But I am using the word 'think', implying he may just be thinking that he smells thus creating doubt in his mind. He picked it up straight away.

'You mean I may just be thinking I smell? I have been to the Doctor's but he doesn't seem interested. He just said, 'There's nothing wrong with you.' I went to the hospital because I had a bad time with my bowel a few years back, but they say there's nothing wrong with my bowel now.' They invalidated his belief too soon that's why he couldn't believe them.

'Is it O.K. if I come over there and smell you?'

'I suppose so.'

I went over to him and sniffed very loudly all over him, leaving nowhere on his body that I might have missed any smell. I smelt body deodorant and talc and nothing else. I told him that I could only smell the talc and deodorant. Notice I still haven't invalidated his belief, but I certainly have dented it.

He said, 'Nobody has ever done that before, are you sure that's all you can smell?'

His asking me if I was sure, let me know he had sufficient doubt and that he was ready for me to undermine his belief that he smelt. I found it hard to believe that someone can go for help, to the doctor and the hospital, because they smell and none of the helpers even take the bother to have a good smell of him. They all told him there was nothing wrong with him, but he obviously interpreted that to mean, 'There is no reason why you smell.' It seems nobody said, 'You don't smell.' I said, **'I wouldn't be able to smell the talc and deodorant if you really smelt awful, would I?'**

'No! because I thought the smell was a stale, horrible, foul smell all over me. They told me it was.'

'Who told you?'

'My friends at school. It became so embarrassing I couldn't go to school. That's why I left and there's no way I could go back. I did quite well in my 'O' levels and was going on to do my 'A's but I got so scared I had to leave. I haven't been able to go for any interviews for a job because I was afraid of smelling. I haven't dared try to get a girlfriend because she would smell me. In fact it is ruining my life.'

'With friends like that who need enemies? Children have a perverse delight in seeing people squirm you know. You gave them a very powerful weapon to hurt you with, the time you showed them you could be hurt and embarrassed by thinking you smelt. Why do you think they always laugh at you? It was not because you smelt but because they found it funny to see you so embarrassed.' Their internal pictures were obviously very different from Pete's, so their truths were also different. If only they could have seen Pete's truth I'm sure they couldn't have been so cruel. [The problem is most people are so involved with their own truth, they can't see any other. I'm sure this is the main problem with most interpersonal difficulties].

'Do you really think so?'

'Well I don't smell anything except talc and deodorant on you, and if you smelt so badly I wouldn't be able to smell those things would I?'

'I suppose not. I feel much better now.'

I had temporarily destroyed his belief but had to do more to stop it coming back. By now he would have built many anchors round his belief that would bring it back if we didn't do anything about them, but he was ready to do something about those anchors now. It's no good trying to do anything about them while he still has his belief, people will defend their beliefs to the death, unless you're subtle about how you tackle them.

So I asked him to tell me how he had made those beliefs seem real. **'What did he do to believe he smelt? What did he do first thing in the morning when he woke up? When did he first think about smelling?'**

He said, 'When I get up I have a bath and it is not long after when I think, am I smelling yet?'

'How do you do that? Do you say to yourself, Do I smell yet?'

'Yes I think I do say that.'

'Do you also see, in your mind, your friends sniffing and laughing at you?'

'Yes I see them running away and calling me smelly.'

'Right, now we know what you do to think you smell, we can change what you think.'

'Thank God for that, you don't know what a nightmare it has all been.'

I told him about the slide change and first asked him to make an auditory change. In the first image he was to hear himself saying to himself, 'I wonder if I smell yet?' and as quickly as he could he was to change the image to picturing himself in bright colour and clear focus, with a sparkle about him, saying to himself, 'What a beautiful morning, this talc and deodorant smells good.' He was to close his eyes to say this and then open them as soon as he said the second image. I then asked him to say it quicker and make the change instantaneously, closing his eyes to say it and opening them as soon as he was finished. The next time he was to leave the last word out from the first image but to say all the second image. [I'm talking about auditory images here]. Then the next time leave another word out from the first and so on until there were no words left to say in the first image. As there were six words in the first image it took six changes to be left with only the second image. I then had him say the second auditory image another three times on its own. Then I asked him to say the first thing again and see what happened. He reported that the second image came in before he had finished saying the first. This is what I needed to know.

Then I had him do a visual slide change. The first picture was taken by him with a black and white film, slightly out of focus, of his friends sniffing and running away. The second slide which was to replace the first immediately, was taken by someone else, so he was in the picture. This picture was in full colour, clear focus, with a sparkle, of him meeting his friends full of confidence and feeling happy to be with them, talking and enjoying just being with them. He was to close his eyes to do this and open them as soon as he had made the last picture and do it as quickly as he could. I asked him to repeat this six times while I counted the six times for him so that he could concentrate on making the pictures. After he had done it six times, I asked him what happened if he tried to just make the first picture and he again reported the second picture came in before he had time to make a full picture of the first. That was all I needed to know.

I met Pete ten weeks after his first visit. He had got a job, and was socializing now by going out with his friends. He still at times wondered if he smelt but that didn't stop him from beginning to enjoy his life a little more. I did a reverse film of the first incident where he was accused of smelling and a double mirror of his driving his mind. I also had him do a marathon exercise which seemed to give him great pleasure, if his face was anything to go by. I'm sure it won't be long before Pete is a very happy neurotic. We have just looked at how children abuse each other, let us now look at how adults abuse children. I was going down to London by train the other day and in the same carriage there was a family, husband, wife, daughter and son, sitting opposite me. The daughter was a delightful little girl, about three years old, with big brown eyes. She kept jumping out of her seat and running to me and climbing on my knee and touching my beard. Somehow she found it fascinating. I didn't mind, she was such a delightful little thing. Her brother, who was only about three years older, was obviously getting a little jealous of all the attention she was attracting. He wanted to get some attention for himself, so he started to fidget and jump about. His mother kept telling him to stop. [At least he was getting some attention]. But he obviously wanted more, so he didn't stop. In the end his mother said to him in a very aggressive voice, 'James! you are a big boy now, behave or you'll get a smack.' The look on James's face told me he didn't see himself as a big boy, after all he was only about six years old. His mother's need from James was for him to behave. His need was to get some attention and relieve his boredom, his sister was having fun so I'm sure James thought, 'Why can't I have some fun?' Neither James nor his mother, however, could see each other's needs. James carried on trying to have some fun and get attention and his mother became more annoyed. James got a smack and didn't want to show how it hurt so he sulked. I'm sure if James had got just a little attention the situation could have been handled better. His mother's need was for James to be a big boy, which he wasn't. James obviously didn't see himself as a big boy and he needed some attention like his sister. Neither of them got what they needed. It's so easy to do things like that, I'm sure we all do similar things and don't notice it.

Once again the problem lies in people having their own internal processing in order to think. No two people have exactly the same processing so no one thinks the same. As Kierkegaard said, 'Whenever we translate 'what is' into words or thoughts there is always a distortion of 'what is'.' The trouble is we believe our distortion to be THE TRUTH. When two people's distortion is different because of their different internal processing, their TRUTHS are different. When that happens abuse is easy to inflict without even being aware of doing it.

A much more serious form of child abuse by adults is having a great amount of publicity in all the media outlets at the moment. I refer to the Cleveland child abuse crisis. To many adults the thought of any adult interfering sexually, in any way, with a defenceless child is utterly abhorrent. I'm sure it is equally abhorrent to most adults to think of another adult physically harming a child to the point of near death, or even death. Yet both forms of abuse are far more widespread than any of us even wish to think. I'm sure it's not just in Cleveland that things like that happen, neither is it just in isolated places. It is widespread all over the globe and has been going on since time began. It's not a new phenomenon, it's just being publicized more now.

The trouble is that the publicity has also made many of the people responsible for dealing with it over-react to the point where they are abusing the children themselves, without even realizing it and in the assumption that they are doing the right thing for the child. I'm sure the doctors responsible for diagnosing abuse have their own truth and justify that truth even to the point of abusing the children themselves, in order to do so. I'm sure the Members of Parliament involved in helping the parents and children have their truths and reasons for what they are doing, and will defend their truths and reasons, even to the point of abusing either the parents or the children in doing so. I'm sure the social workers believe in their truths, in what they are doing for the children, and will defend their truths even to the point of abusing the children themselves and not even know they are doing it. I'm sure the media is trying to do it's bit in exposing this atrocity by over-exposing it, never realizing that they are also causing abuse by their behaviour.

Nobody can condone child abuse. Whenever I come across a case of abuse seeking help I always think, 'Oh no! Not again.' The trouble is that most of the people trying to help with abuse are helping from their own truths and in doing so are certainly abusing the children with their distorted truths, in an attempt to help, even if the children were or were not abused in the first place. There seems to be considerable doubt about whether the children were abused by their parents in the first place. There can be no doubt that they are being abused by what all the do gooders are doing in an attempt to help. I believe all the publicity and so-called help has put the treatment of child abuse back into the dark ages. Normal parents are almost frightened to show parental love to their children in case they get arrested. Children are frightened to tell, in case they get taken away in the middle of the night. Parents are frightened to take their children to the hospital for any treatment in case their children are wrongly diagnosed as suffering from child abuse. I'm sure many of us are glad our children are grown up, because we wonder if our normal way of showing our children that we loved and cared for them would be construed as abuse.

The biggest problem, as I see it, is that no-one seems to be bothered about WHY an adult abuses a child, or even has any idea how to find out how they could do such a thing. Similarly, no-one seems to have any idea how to treat and help an abuser to change. The only treatment seems to lock the abuser away where they can't do it, at least until they are let out again, when the whole horrible process starts all over again.

No-one seems to know how to help someone who has been abused to change the way they think about themselves, after they have been abused. Even many years after they have been abused, when they have got away from the person who was abusing them and may even have met and settled with a loving person, the abused person often displays a wide range of inhibiting behaviours which make them unhappy. It seems to me it is imperative for everyone concerned with child abuse to get together and try to see each other's truth before we will be in a position to really help. Both abused and abuser, doctor, social worker, M.P., Parliament, the police and all the other people involved should find a way to help abusers and abused to change what they do and think, otherwise this problem will grow out of all proportion. Holding their own truths as 'THE TRUTH' will only worsen the situation. Every day, in the media, you can see one of the people involved defending their position as 'right', totally neglecting the fact that their defence may be harming the children.

I have helped a number of abused people to change what

they think about themselves, thus enabling them to live happier and normal lives. I quote a case in my book, 'It's a Bit of a Mouthful', in the chapter on oral sex. In fact that chapter is all about an adult who was abused as a child.

Another case I helped, was the wife of a professional friend. My friend asked me to see if I could help his wife who was depressed and suicidal. He loved his wife and she loved him, they had everything going for them. They had no real financial problems. They had two lovely children and a comfortable home. His job was secure and gave him enough time to be with his wife. They had good friends with whom they socialized and to an outsider there was absolutely nothing that should have made his wife depressed. In fact she felt all the more guilty and unworthy for being depressed and suicidal, as she couldn't think of any reason why she should be as she was. She did have a fear that she would in some way hurt her children. She also disliked her father and was a little afraid of him. He interfered with their life and wasn't very good to her mother. They were always having rows. She said whenever they came to visit she didn't know what would happen. Her husband was very tolerant with them but she wished her father wouldn't come to visit because they always argued when they came.

She was diagnosed as a classical case of endogenous depression and prescribed anti-depressants. They didn't seem to help. She saw a psychiatrist who didn't help. The psychiatrist was suggesting it was to do with the relationship between her husband and herself. As this didn't fit with either her truth or her husband's they thought it was a waste of time going to see him. So my friend turned to me to see if I could help. Lynn was an attractive, thirty-five year old intelligent lady, who, as I said earlier, had everything going for her except that she was suicidal. She hadn't actually ever done anything to take her life but she had sat and looked at her wrists for about half an hour with a sharp knife in her hand. She had also been to a cliff top and looked down for about the same time, wondering if she dared to jump. Fortunately she was too scared to do either, as she had also been when she looked at a bottle of analgesic pills and wondered if she should swallow the lot.

She didn't like taking the anti-depressants as they made her sleepy and not 'with it', so she had come off them by herself. She couldn't think of anything that could be the reason for her feeling the way she did. She didn't particularly like herself and thought she wasn't a very nice person or a good mother. I'm sure her children loved her. I am equally sure she hadn't done anything to her children to make her feel she wasn't a good mother. She felt guilty about the way she felt about her father, and sorry for her mother. She had a normal sexual relationship with her husband, but sometimes she just did it because he wanted it. Her mother was sometimes depressed and nervous. Her father was always aggressive.

She was a high capacity hypnotic subject with little or no resistance. I believe that there is a reason for every behaviour, even endogenous depression. I do not follow the theory that endogenous depression is always a psychotic illness due to a bio-chemical imbalance. There may be an imbalance but there is a reason for the imbalance which is unconscious. Because of my belief I decided to try to explore her unconscious mind to find a reason for her depression. I set up an ideo-finger response and asked Lynn a number of questions concerning the things discussed above in my description of this case. When we came to ask, had her father, who she had said she was afraid of, anything to do with her depression we got a strong 'Yes' answer. I followed this up with the question, **'Are you strong enough at this point in time to let your conscious mind know what your father has to do with your depression?'** Before I got the answer I thought 'Oh no! here we go again.' Her finger said, 'No.' [She wasn't strong enough, or she wasn't ready yet, to know]. If that is the case you will only lose your patient if you try to continue, so I decided to leave well alone for the time being. I did know that it must be something with a great deal of emotion attached, otherwise she wouldn't be running away from finding out. I followed, however, in this session with the question, **'Was there sometime in the future when she would be strong enough and ready to know what he had**

to do with her depression?' Her finger said 'Yes.'

At her next visit she said she had had a blazing row with her father. He and her mother had come to Lynn's house for the evening. As soon as Lynn saw her father she felt aggressive towards him. She thought this strange as she usually felt a little afraid of him, he usually made her feel like a little girl. Her father and mother started to argue almost as soon as they arrived. She found herself saying, 'For goodness sake, if you are going to be like that, go back home.' This shocked Lynn, because she had wanted to say something like that to him for years but had never dared to open her mouth when he was present. He continued with his raveing so she went and got his coat and hat, made him put it on and she pushed him out the door. She was shaking all over, she wasn't sure if it was with rage or shock at her bravery in taking a stand. It was probably both. Afterwards she phoned her mother to apologize and to explain it was her father she objected to.

Obviously whatever we had begun to unearth at her last appointment had had an effect even when her unconscious mind thought she wasn't strong enough to know about it consciously. Whenever you start something moving in your unconscious it will make changes in you, even when you don't know how. That's how metaphors work. I explained how she could go on for the rest of her life making slow changes, like the one that had just happened the last time her father had come to her house, or she could find out what he had done to make her depressed and get it out of the way once and for all. I said she may find afterwards she could have a different relationship with her father but it probably would be a better one and be more real. There is no reason why an adult woman should be afraid of anyone let alone her father. I asked her if she would like to try again with the ideo-motor questioning. She said, 'Yes.'

I set it up and this time when I asked her unconscious mind if she was strong enough at this moment in time to know consciously what her father had done to make her depressed, her finger answered, 'YES.' I used an 'affect bridge' to make it conscious. This is a technique I often use. It entails a process whereby the patient becomes more and more aware of the suppressed hurt inside their system [Body and Mind]. It goes something like the following. **'Whatever your father did to make you depressed it must have hurt you. At that time, you probably shut off the hurt and tried to feel alright, but the hurt is still inside you, making you depressed now. Let yourself feel the hurt so that it may come out and as it was long ago when you were hurt, you'll be able to let go of it, with the effect that it won't go on hurting you now that it is all over. To hold on to that hurt, even though it is only in your unconscious, is making you depressed, it's just not worth it. [If it wasn't over she would still remember it consciously]. You feel hurt in your stomach, in your eyes, in your chest. In fact you feel hurt all over your body and mind.'** She was squirming in the chair and breathing very heavily. There were tears in her eyes and she obviously felt very uncomfortable. I encouraged her to go on feeling the hurt and let it build up. As she became more upset I said, **'Let that hurt take you to the time when it was being inflicted upon you. Go back in time and feel you are being hurt now.'** [This is the 'affect bridge', using the feelings to bridge time to take a person back to when the feelings were being formulated in the first place].

She began to sob heavily and say, 'No! No! it's not happening. It's not true.' Saying, 'No' is trying to dissociate from it. She may well have dissociated from it, as a defence, even while it was happening, with the result that while it was happening it seemed unreal to her. This makes it easier to forget consciously that it ever happened. But because it did happen it still goes into the unconscious mind as an unfelt feeling threatening to be felt and making her depressed. It also makes her feel a bad person because, with dissociation, there is always some doubt as to whether it really happened, even when it did happen, with the result that the person will then blame themselves, perhaps thinking they just made it up. This makes them feel guilty for thinking such a terrible thing about someone they should love. It also, naturally, interferes with the abused person's ability to love someone who they feel they should love. It may even get in the way of them loving anyone properly. It makes the abused person have a different internal processing when it comes to them thinking about love. Their 'Truth' about love, most probably, will be even more distorted, than someone who wasn't abused. In any case it will be different, and this may well create problems with their interpersonal relationships, even with their own children. An abused person is more likely to abuse their own children because their own children will trigger off this suppressed hurt in their parents unconscious, with the result that the parent may blame the children for hurting them and want to hurt their children back.

'What is not happening?'

'My father is interfering with me, he is trying to make love to me, it's hurting. I'm telling him to get off, but he won't. Afterwards he is saying that if I tell anyone he will be taken away, then what will happen to my mother and I? He said if that happened he would kill me before they took him away.'

No wonder she forgot all about it. It was too frightening to remember. I had Lynn do a zoom picture of this. In the first picture she saw herself as a small child being abused by her father, which she zoomed away until it was just a blur, then she brought back a full colour picture of herself as an adult telling her father where to get off, just as she had done during the week before this appointment. She was to remember how she had pushed him out and how feeble he looked. She did a zoom of being in control with her in the back seat in the first picture and then her in the driving seat of her mind in the zoom picture. She did the marathon telling herself she had as much right as anyone to be here on this earth.

She became much more assertive in her life and her depression lifted. To my knowledge it hasn't returned in five years. I'm sure she would have come back if it had. She, in the end, could feel pity for her father, he was probably abused by his father, but he got no help with it. She ceased to be a patient and has become a friend.

Another case I helped was a man who had been abused by both his parents. Generally it's the father who abuses the child. This is a case of a 34 year old man who had been prosecuted for exposing himself to young children. His solicitor phoned me to say that the court had ordered his client to have treatment for his offence. The offender had seen a psychiatrist but still felt an uncontrollable urge to expose himself to children. If he didn't get help soon he felt sure he would get caught doing it again, and this time he would get a much stiffer sentence.

He was a single man living by himself in his own home. He had a good steady job but didn't go out socially. He had no friends to speak of, and occasionally went to the pub for a drink but found it difficult to socialize even after he had had a few drinks. He said whenever he saw young children playing by themselves he had this terrible urge to expose himself to them. He found himself going to the park where children were playing and waiting to see if any children were alone, without their parents or adults. He had exposed himself about a dozen times before getting caught. He had once tried to make love to a prostitute but hadn't been able to manage it. The prostitute had been kind and told him not to worry. He hadn't ever had a girlfriend.

He had admitted his previous offences in court, but his solicitor got him off with a probation order, as this was his client's first prosecution for offence. This decision for probation only, was provided his client received treatment. The problem was where to get treatment that would help. There seem to be very few places where someone with this sort of difficulty can get any help that is of any use. Perhaps this is one thing the authorities should look at in the child abuse dilemma. I feel one of the main difficulties is in finding trained therapists who understand the problem and have any ability in helping people to make changes in their behaviour. This is another reason for my writing this book.

I asked him about his childhood and his relationship with his parents. His father had been in the navy when he was small and because of this he didn't see much of his father. He was away on some ship most of the time. When his father was away my patient slept in the same bed as his mother. When his father came home he was booted out of his mother's bed into the other bedroom where it was cold and frightening. He was afraid of his father who seemed to resent his being there. He often got physically beaten by his father for being cheeky. [Probably he felt his nose pushed out when he had to get out of his mother's bed, and was seeking attention. His 'Truths' were obviously different to his father's].

My patient remembers touching his mother's breasts when he thought she was asleep and on a few occasions he was sure she was only pretending she was asleep. She touched him a few times between his legs and he pretended to be asleep and once when he had got very aroused she had put his penis into her, but he had come almost as soon as she did it. She had pushed him off and told him to get out of the bed into his own bed in the other room. She had let him come back into her bed the next night though and had touched him again when she thought he had been asleep. She never again tried to put his penis into her.

Then, when he was about eleven, his father came home and didn't go back to sea. He was condemned and dismissed from his mother's bed for ever and he hated his father. His mother seemed to prefer her husband so she didn't love my patient any more. He hated her for her fickleness. He couldn't wait to get away from them both. As soon as a situation presented itself he left and went away to work, away from home.

We found in his unconscious mind he hated adults and felt he couldn't trust them. They would as soon hurt you as look at you. He couldn't frighten them so he frightened little children by exposing himself to them. They screamed and ran away when he did it. That made him feel big. Exposing himself also made him feel big. The children could see his penis was big. Actually he thought he had a small one but it was bigger than the children's so they thought it was big. It would be too frightening to show it to an adult because they would think it was only small and useless. His mother had more or less said that, when she told him to go to his own bed when he had ejaculated prematurely with her. The prostitute had confirmed he was useless when he tried it with her. He hated her even though she hadn't done anything to make him feel that way.

The internal processes he used in thinking were being affected very badly by all these experiences. He felt small and useless most of the time, in fact the only time he felt big and strong was when he exposed himself to children and they screamed and ran away. He felt good then. No wonder, his feelings of inferiority just built up all the time until he had to expose himself to feel big and strong and good.

We had to re-write the endings of most of his stories about his mother and father. We had to re-write the endings of the stories about little boy's penises and adult's penises. We had to re-write the ending to the stories about little children thinking adults' penises were big and that made adults think they were big. We had to do a zoom about who was driving my patient. His compulsion to expose himself when he saw young children was the basis of his first picture which, when zoomed away, changed into a little boy feeling unloved and unhappy which was zoomed farther away until it was just a blur. The picture zoomed back was of my patient big and strong not needing little children to confirm that he was an adult, who could be friendly with children or adults, with no desire to make a fool of himself with either.

We had him do a double mirror exercise with a sad little boy who misunderstood the circumstances around him when he was small and vulnerable in the mirror behind him. Then in the mirror in front he saw his cured adult self, big and colourful, socializing with other adults. [His cured self was no longer compelled to get false security from little children by exposing himself]. When he smiled as he was imagining this self he was encouraged to step right into the mirror and then open his eyes. He did the zoom slides and double mirror exercises until the second images became a compulsion. He also did these exercises with a change in the internal dialogue about the pictures until the internal dialogue he wanted became a compulsion.

So far as I know he hasn't exposed himself since, or even wanted to. He is getting better at socializing but he recognizes it is difficult for a 35 year old man who hasn't got any friends to suddenly make a lot of real friends, but he is trying.

In this chapter so far we've looked at how children abuse children and how adults abuse children, so now look at how adults abuse other adults. I heard a true story the other day of such an abuse that amazed me. The wife of a friend of mine had been shopping with her children and had left them in one shop, happily looking at something they wanted to see, while she went into another to change an item she had bought the day before which didn't fit her. She spent rather longer than she had intended in this second shop so, getting worried about her children, she ran out to see if they were still alright. She slipped while running and twisted her ankle badly. She managed to hobble to her children and then drive her car home. As she arrived at the house in great pain, thinking she was now safely home, instead of putting her injured foot on the brake she somehow put it on the accelerator and accidentally drove the car into the garage wall, doing quite a bit of damage to the car. The next day, as her ankle was no better, she went to the hospital and was told her ankle was badly sprained and to keep off it as much as possible and walk with a pair of crutches which she was given.

She phoned another friend of mine the next day, to see if she could take her to the hospital the following morning as she had been instructed to return for a check up on her ankle. She said her husband had said her sprained ankle was all her fault and was sheer carelessness on her part. She shouldn't have run in the shop in the first place. She shouldn't have driven her car and she wouldn't have caused the damage to her car and garage wall in the second place. So, as it was all her fault, she could get the bus to the hospital for her check up as he wouldn't take her. She said to my other friend it would be so difficult getting into the bus with crutches.

The lady with the sprained ankle obviously had her 'Truth' about how it all happened, while her husband seemed to have an entirely different 'Truth' about the whole affair. As their 'Truths' were so different my friend had no difficulty in abusing his wife, without even realizing it. He felt perfectly justified in teaching her a lesson for doing what he saw as pure carelessness. I will add he relented in the end and saw it, at least partly, her way. I hope this example, however, shows how easy it is for one adult to abuse another without even realizing it and we all are guilty of doing it at one time or another, so don't kid yourself that you are perfect and could never do anything like that, because you would be wrong. When we do do things like that, however, we cause a great deal of unhappiness. Many people, unfortunately, don't have the necessary skill to put it right afterwards and only make it worse by trying to defend their first judgement. Because of their personal internal processing they find it difficult to admit they may have been wrong. When you learn to change that processing it becomes easier to put it right and make everybody happier. Remember human insult causes self destruct processes to occur. If you insult someone you end up, more often than not, destroying yourself.

It is very easy, at this point in time, to see in professional sport how human insult is spoiling the game. Everyone seems to be defending their insults as justifiable, to the detriment of the game. And it's not only in sport, you can see this sort of behaviour every time you pick up a newspaper. It is full of people defending their behaviour by insulting someone else. So long as we go on doing that the world becomes sadder and the people in it become unhappier. Suicide becomes commonplace and death, destruction and abuse occur all the more.

Another very common form of abuse, which occurs between two adults, which seems to become more and more widespread every day, occurs when one or other of the adults falls out of love with the other. I was reading in a newspaper only the other day that, 'Women find men aggressive, emotional cripples, who never listen to their women, try to dominate them in thought, word and deed, make their wives and lovers feel like housemaids.' The paper went on to say that, '70% of women married for five years or more have extra-marital affairs and the majority of these don't feel guilty about it.' I'm sure the same sort of figures of unfaithfulness will apply to men, if not more.

Each one is often so busy trying to justify their own behaviour, so that they don't feel guilty, that they cannot see the other's 'Truth', so they abuse the other. I have heard a number of guilty partners accuse the other of trying to make them feel guilty and blaming their partner for their unfaithful behaviour so that they don't have to feel guilty. Guilt, or the defence a person may fabricate to not feel guilty, seems to cloud the whole issue and becomes a big stumbling block when they may try to get together again.

It is my belief, when there is a break-up between two people, if there are young children involved, that every effort should be made to get the people involved, together again. If they once loved each other enough to marry and wanted to have children to each other, they can be changed to have an even better relationship with each other than they had before they split up. It is no good going back to the relationship they had before the break-up because that relationship led to the break-up. Often you hear of people saying, 'We are trying to get back together.' I always say, **'That's no good. It didn't work. Why don't we see if we can get you forward together to something better than you had?'**

Whenever I have treated both people involved in a break-up, provided they both wanted to get involved with each other again, I have so far never failed to find a way to help them to have a better relationship than they ever had, even before the break-up.

The two main things you have to get out of the way before you can do that is the guilt, either conscious or unconscious guilt and to stop each partner playing the blame game. Who cares who's fault it is, what they both need to do is to be able to see each other's 'Truth' and see how each of their, 'truths' are different. Then all you need to do is to find a way for both of them to change their 'truths' so that they are nearer to each other. All that is technically possible when there is a wish on both sides.

The best way to get the guilt and blame game out of the way is to explain that when someone is in love with someone else they are temporarily insane. When they fall out of love they are again temporarily insane. In between they love each other. [See Chapter 3]. Let's find a way to make you both sane about each other. Being in love is a temporary state and being out of love is also a temporary state. When you are in love you can only see the object of your love in a good light and you distort all your 'truths' to do that. You can't distort all your 'truths' for ever outside of an asylum. When you fall out of love you distort all your 'truths' so that you see only the bad side of someone, and you can't do that forever either. If you once have both been attracted to each other there must be something in both of your 'truths' that can meet. All you have to do is to find out what that is and build on it.

You can use any or all of the techniques discussed in Chapter 4, and again in the next chapter, to change people's beliefs and when you make their beliefs nearer to each other they become much happier with each other. You have to be aware of the difficulties discussed in the next chapter before you can change beliefs and leave a person whole. It is possible, however, to make anyone who once loved someone else to love them again, hopefully in a better way so that it will last. It will last if both partners want it to. People don't change that much without help, they all exhibit stuck states. Many people in break-up situations justify the break-up by saying we've both changed. More often than not they haven't changed, the only thing that has changed is the way they think about each other. Anyhow, anybody can be anything they want when they know how and are prepared to change.

Now finally, while we are dealing with abuse let us look at how an adult may abuse themselves. Jack was referred to me by his doctor. Jack had been to hospital to have half of his lung removed because of lung cancer. [See Chapter 3]. He had been told about cigarette smoking and how that was responsible for his lung cancer, yet Jack still smoked 20 to 40 cigarettes a day. He couldn't work as a taxi driver because he couldn't stop coughing when he smoked and as he smoked well over 20 cigarettes every day that meant he was smoking most of the time. He said he didn't want to die and all his family loved him and were trying to help him stop smoking and still he put one cigarette into his mouth after the other.

I asked Jack, **'How did he do that? How did he put one cigarette after another into his mouth and light it when he said he wanted to stop smoking? What did he do to himself to make him do that?'** You could hardly impress the dangers of smoking on Jack any more than he already knew. He had already lost half his lung with cancer caused by smoking. He had a terrible cough so he must know the other half of his lungs were objecting to his smoking. So he must do something very strongly to himself to have to keep on smoking. **'What was it that he did that made him smoke?'**

Jack didn't know, if he had known I'm sure he would have stopped before having to come and see me. I asked him to imagine he was just getting up in the morning and asked him, **'What was he doing to want a cigarette?'**

He said, 'Oh I wake up early and I get up to have a smoke then I go back to bed.'

'What do you say to yourself when you wake up, to want a cigarette?'

'When I wake up I think to myself I would love a cigarette. I've always smoked ever since I was about eight years old. I look forward to the first one in the morning. I have never smoked in bed, so I get up to have one.'

'You say you want to stop smoking and yet you tell yourself you would love a cigarette as soon as you wake up. What is that saying to your mind?'

'I suppose it's saying go on have one.'

'Yes it is. So your mind then says O.K. I'll help you, 'Get up out of bed and have a cigarette before I have to stop you.' You are in a programme by this time and your mind will do almost anything to help you to complete that programme. Nothing you do or tell yourself after you have told yourself you would love a cigarette can stop you while you are in that programme.'

'Yes that's right, I just feel I have to have one.'

'After you have one what happens then?'

'I go back to bed and about an hour later I get up and have a cup of tea and perhaps some breakfast. Then I see the cigarettes on the table where I left them and I think I'd love another.'

'**You tell yourself when you notice your cigarettes on the table to have another.**'

'I suppose so. I sometimes manage not to have one straight away but fairly soon I have to have one, or I begin to feel restless or irritated.'

'**You mean your mind is so intent in helping you to have what you have just told yourself to have that it makes you irritated if you resist. It gives you an excuse to have one**'

'Now you point it out I suppose that's right. I hadn't thought of it like that before you pointed it out.'

'**So you have another cigarette, then when do you want another?**'

'It can be any time, I just think I haven't had a cigarette for some time so why don't I have another one? I can be doing anything, or often when I have just finished one thing before I start the next, I'll want one.'

'**So you have another and if you resist you feel irritated again.**'

'Yes that's about it.'

'**Now what is the first thing you see when you are about to have a cigarette?**'

'I suppose it's the cigarette in my hand coming towards my mouth.'

'**When you no longer are being controlled by chopped up dried leaves, rolled into a stick with a piece of paper, and feel quite comfortable when you don't have a cigarette any more, will you feel any better about yourself as a person? Won't it be nice to be in control yourself and not have to rely on dried leaves to be comfortable?**'

'Yes I will feel much better.' That's all I needed to know.

'**O.K. so now let us do something that is going to help you be a non-smoker. I want you to imagine you are in the middle of a cinema sitting comfortably waiting for the film to begin. Before the film starts I want you to imagine you can take your mind out of your body and take it to the back of the cinema where your mind can watch your body watching the film while your body is sitting in the middle of the cinema. [This creates a dissociated feeling from the** film while Jack watches the film]. When your mind is at the back, watching your body watch the film, the film can start. It is an old film in black and white and is as if it is seen from your eyes. It starts when you are waking up in the morning and you see the bedroom as you get up. You are not fully in the film because it is what you see from out of your eyes. You go down stairs and take a cigarette in your hand and you see it coming towards your mouth in your hand. Then you see yourself light the cigarette and the end of the cigarette glows red then some smoke drifts upwards into the air. At this point the film stops and you see your body get up from the middle of the cinema and go right up to the screen. Then your body steps into the film and the picture changes to full colour. When this happens the film starts again but this time it runs backwards. Everything in the film runs backwards and this time you are fully in the film. [Associated fully with what is in the film by being in it]. You see the smoke coming back down to the cigarette, the red glow going out, the match going out, your hand going back down to the packet and putting the cigarette back instead of taking it out. Yourself walking backwards up the stairs to your bedroom and reversing into bed. 'Were you able to see all that?''

'Yes.'

'Good! Now do that film and the reverse film all over again as quickly as you can. Don't take more than a few seconds over it. Remember you are not in the forward film, it is as if it is seeing it all out of your eyes but you are in the reverse film.'

He did it in about ten seconds. Then we did the same about the next time he had told me he had a cigarette and each time, until we finished up with him sitting with friends and having a cigarette and reversing that so he was putting the cigarette back in the packet and not smoking. When he had done all that I asked him if he felt like having a cigarette.

He said, 'Not at the moment.'

I asked him if he had any cigarettes on him but he didn't have any. I don't smoke, nor does any of my staff in the building. If he had had one on him I would have asked him to look at it and see if he felt like having a cigarette when he saw one. Unfortunately my next patient was waiting by this time, so I made Jack another appointment in two weeks' time.

When he came back in two weeks time he looked quite pleased with himself. He said he had only smoked about ten cigarettes in the two weeks. I said that was ten too many, but it was a start. He would normally have smoked between 300 to 550 in that time. I congratulated him on not smoking over 290 cigarettes and said as he had given up at least 290 cigarettes in two weeks he would find it much easier to give up ten in two weeks. He said he had been fine for the first week, then when he had gone to the pub at the weekend and he smelt cigarettes he had had one. After that he had had the odd one to make it ten in the two weeks.

I did the reverse film again and then I did a series of slide changes. In the first film he saw his bedroom as he woke up in the morning and said to himself, 'I would love a cigarette.' Then in the change he saw himself waking up in the morning saying to himself, 'I'm so pleased with myself that I don't smoke any more. It's good to be in control of myself'. He did that six times missing another word off the first slide each time he did it, until he only said the words in the last slide the last time. When I asked him to make an image of the first slide only, he said he couldn't, the second one came in automatically. He did a slide change of seeing his cup of tea and saying to himself, 'I would love a cigarette.' Then the changed slide of him having his cup of tea and saying, 'I can enjoy the taste of this tea much better without having a cigarette.' Once again he did it until he had a compulsion to see the second slide. Then we did a slide change of having a pint of beer with his friends, while he could smell cigarettes and saying to himself, 'I will just have one.' In the change he could see himself with his friends having a pint and smelling cigarettes all round him while he said to himself, 'Thank goodness I don't smoke. Cigarettes smell like burning leaves because that is all they are.' This ended up a compulsion after he had done it six times.

I made him an appointment for a month's time but he rang

up a week before his appointment and said, 'Would I mind if he didn't come, because he hadn't had any cigarettes at all since he last saw me, and he couldn't see himself ever smoking again.' He lived quite a long way away and as he had given me enough warning that he didn't want the appointment I thought it quite reasonable for him not to come. It meant someone else could have his appointment. I'm always busy and generally have someone waiting for a cancellation.

I hope this chapter shows you why it is so easy for someone to abuse another human being and gives you some pointers how to help someone to change. When they do change everybody connected with them becomes happier.

CHAPTER 6

Peoples Truths: How to change them

One of the wonderful things about being involved in Psychotherapy is that you get to meet quite a lot of wonderful people, feeling people, people who care for their fellow man. Whenever you attend a course or workshop in psychotherapy, there are always people of like mind to be found there. There is a saying that there is nothing new under the sun. You work in your own little patch on this earth and think you have discovered something new, then you meet fellow travellers and find they have similar discoveries. One of those people for me is my old friend Bill Pemberton and his delightful wife Oma, who live in Mill Valley, California. We met one year long ago, when Bill and Oma were over in England. They had been told to contact me when they came to England. I don't know who told them but I will be eternally grateful. A mutual friend says of us, we just go together like 'Holmes and Watson.' [See below the cartoon he drew of us at the Sherlock Holmes meeting].

The three of us were attending a Sherlock Holmes meeting in San-Francisco with our wives. I am telling you all this because when people meet with similar 'truths' something wonderful happens, and everybody involved feels happier and enriched. Another person who always enriches my life is David Cheek, who is also from San-Francisco. We met at a Workshop that I was giving in San-Francisco and we both knew instantly that we could get on together. I have learned so much from both of these two wonderful people.

It was Bill who introduced me to the work of Alfred Korzybski. Bill had actually worked with Korzybski. Bill also introduced me to the work of Richard Bandler as he had been on some of the earlier workshops which Richard Bandler had given. Over the years we have known each other Bill has always said, 'One of the hardest things to do on this planet is talk meaningfully with someone with a different sacred system.'

I believe it is this recognizing of similar truths that first sparks off an attraction between two people. That's why I believe when two people meet and fall in love, marry and have children by each other, even when it appears that all is lost between them, or when one or both say we've changed, if both have a will to move forward together, it is always possible to save the marriage and make it better than it has ever been, both for the couple and their children. When, however, two people meet and their beliefs are so far apart that they cannot see any mutual 'truths', communication between them is almost impossible. Getting back, however, to what Bill Pemberton says, 'One of the hardest things to do on this planet is talk meaningfully with someone with a different sacred system'. This could be seen very clearly when the Ayatollah Khomeini of Iran had taken American hostages in Iran and President Carter was trying to get them out. They were both insulting each other and if it had been left to them, the hostages would still be there today. In the Sunday Express, 20 Dec.'87, there was an article which starts, 'Crazed Iranian leader Ayatollah Khomeini has named the man who will take over as head of his blood-soaked revolution'. In the article it is pointed out that the new leader is to ensure that,

1. The war against Iraq and in particular 'Zionist infidel' Sadam Hussein must continue to the bitter end;
2. The Saudi Arabian Royal family must be brought down;
3. Israel, the 'Zionist entity,' must be destroyed;
4. The 'Great Satan' embodied in U.S. and Western culture must be resisted at all costs;
5. The Islamic revolution was to be waged globally until all 'evil' was eradicated;
6. The clergy must be the flag-bearers of Iran's armed struggle to impose Islam on to the world.

How does someone who isn't Islamic talk to someone who says all that? To start with I'm sure Khomeini doesn't think he is 'Crazed'. I'm sure Sadam Hussein doesn't think he is an 'Infidel'. I'm sure the Saudi Royal family and the Israeli's don't want to be destroyed. I'm sure the U.S. and Western cultures don't think of themselves as 'Great Satan'. And I'm sure that anyone who isn't Islamic is greatly put off from ever becoming Islamic by what the Ayatollah has just said, so probably thousands of innocent people have to die for a sacred system. One of the other things Bill taught me about 'truths' is that 'Human insults create self destruction.' Whenever you insult someone by invalidating their 'truth' you destroy yourself in the light of the other person.

I'm sure this factor has been a great difficulty in the recent talks and the agreement between Ronald Reagan and Mikhail Gorbachev. We have to congratulate them both, with their countries, in at least being able to see a little of each other's 'truths.' In fact if you pick up a newspaper these days it will be full of situations created by people with different 'truths' where great hostility is the result of neither side being able to see the other person's 'truths'. The whole world seems to be rushing headlong into obliteration because of this problem of communication without insult or without invalidation of 'truths'.

If you watch and listen you will see people all over the globe both insulting one another and invalidating each others 'truths'. Then they start blaming each other, which is just inflicting a second insult, or invalidation. It also is playing the 'blame game' which leads to stuck states and make it impossible to change the situation, while they continue to blame each other. Then they can't understand why all hell is let loose and death and destruction results. If you need an example just look at the situation in Iraq and Iran, or nearer to home in Ireland between Catholic and Protestant. I'm sure you don't need examples, they are all around you everywhere.

Whenever you get Extremist views of any kind, imposing strict 'truths' or beliefs on followers, you can be sure people will end up dead. This is all done in the name of a belief system. The deaths are caused because the people trapped in extreme 'beliefs' cannot see other peoples 'truths' and therefore cannot communicate in a meaningful way with anyone outside their own belief. When that happens you start insulting anybody outside your belief and 'war' breaks out. Nations know this but they seem to be impotent to do anything about it. We do have the skills, but there are too many people entrenched in their self preservation of their 'truths' to be able to use those skills to solve the problems in the world today.

When you take what Kierkegaard said, 'Whenever we translate 'What is' into language or thought, there is always a distortion of 'What is' it seems a little pointless to kill for a distorted 'truth'. Remember, we are distorting 'what is' by our internal processes, but then we have to go and believe the distortion as 'THE TRUTH'.

It is not only in international politics that we see the difficulties discussed earlier in this chapter. These difficulties are all around us, in everyday folk. People are screwing each other up right, left, and centre, everywhere, without even being aware of doing it. When they do invalidate another person's truth or belief a great deal of unhappiness is the result. I hope I have shown you in the last chapter on Abuse how easy it is for one person to abuse another, all because of having different internal processing systems, and therefore different 'truths'. I hope I have also convinced you by now that it is possible to change that internal processing, so that in doing so you also change the persons 'truths'. You have to be careful when you set out to deliberately change peoples 'truths', because in doing so you may lose them before you have done your work.

If you start out from the beginning invalidating a person's beliefs you will very quickly lose rapport. Remember I said one of the essential elements in producing change is rapport. But when someone's belief/truth is resulting in that person being 'Stuck', and the resulting 'stuck state' is crippling them and making them unhappy then you have to help them to change their belief/truth somehow or other. Negative beliefs/truths are the traps that most unhappy neurotics fall into. The trouble then is they will defend even these negative beliefs/truths to the 'death'. For example it is very hard helping someone who thinks they are useless, everytime you do something to help them they ignore your suggestions saying, 'I can't do that!' [See later in Chapter 8, how Eve's truths were preventing her from being happy, and yet she held on to them like grim death]. If a person believes they love someone, even if that someone is making them miserable by their totally unreasonable behaviour, it is very difficult to help the person in love. They will resist almost everything you do to help them and remain unhappy. Everybody else can see why they are unhappy but the person in love refuses to give up their belief. It is possible to help them get over that belief when you can convince them that that is what is making them miserable. The way to help them get over it, when you have shown them it is their belief that is the trouble, is to do a forward and reverse film of their falling in love with that person. When you have done that they will have no feelings for that person. Another way is to create an anchor for their love and then create an anchor for something they hate, then when they are thinking about their loved one fire both anchors. For both these techniques see the next Chapter on phobias.

A way to convince a person that their behaviour is what is crippling them is demonstrated in the following technique which I used with Yvonne and James. They were both having a rough time with each other. She was blaming him for their very shaky marriage and James was blaming her. They both were waiting for the other to make a move to make it better as each believed that it had nothing to do with them, but it was all the other's fault. In doing so, each was miserable and they were succeeding in thoroughly screwing up their two children and making the whole family unhappy. James said to me, 'When my wife behaves in a reasonable manner we will be alright,' and Yvonne said, 'When my husband behaves better I will be alright and able to be more normal'. Neither were able to see that whatever both of them had been doing to each other didn't work, if it had, they wouldn't need to be seeing me.

I began by trying to make Yvonne see the truth, at least to me, that she was creating a no go area for change, by her belief that the only way she would be able to cope with the situation was by being absolutely uptight about it, with the result that whatever James said to her was taken as a personal attack on her. With this attitude of Yvonne's, whatever James said made matters worse. She complained of being sick of the situation, while as she told me this, she let out a loud sigh. I said to her, **'Help me to appreciate how you get so sick of the situation. What is it you do to be so sick of it?'** Notice I haven't invalidated her belief that it is James who is making her sick yet. It's too soon to do that, and if you do at this stage Yvonne will just think you are taking James's side. You have to be neutral to help this sort of situation and don't even try to play the blame game or you'll get nowhere. Then I said, **'Let's pretend that I'm going to be you for today and you are going to have the day off somewhere where you will be more relaxed. I want you to show me exactly how to be so sick of the situation, just like you! What do I have to do first to be you?'**

'Well for a start you just have to grit your teeth and bear it.'

'O.K. so I'm gritting my teeth and bearing it.' Gritting my teeth in an exaggerated manner and letting out an exaggerated sigh. **'That's a bit uncomfortable, but what else do I have to do to be you?'**

'You have to hang on to survive.'

'I have to hang on to survive do I? What will happen if I don't hang on?'

'Well you will lose your sanity, won't you?'

'Oh! will I? O.K. I have to grit my teeth and bear it [sighing] and I have to hang on to keep my sanity. That's even harder and more uncomfortable. No wonder you are sick of it I'm sure I would be sick of it too. How do I hang on to my sanity? What do I have to do to do that?'

'You have to be uptight all the time and be on your guard.'

'Oh! I have to grit my teeth and bear it [Sighing loudly]. I have to be uptight all the time to hang on to my sanity. I have to be on my guard all the time. How do I be on my guard all the time?'

'Well you have to be even more uptight and don't take anything James says at face value.'

'I see! So I have to take everything James says and see if it is in any way critical of me, do I?'

'Yes! It probably will be.'

'So everything James says will be critical of me, will it? So I can expect everything he says to be against me? How am I going to cope with that? I will have made everything James says into an attack on me before he even says anything. No wonder I have to grit my teeth and bear it [Sighing even louder]. No wonder I have to hang on to my sanity by being unbearably uptight. No wonder I have to be always on my guard. But doing all that I'm going to be shattered by the end of the day. Don't you find that?'

'Yes I am!'

'Tell me, I don't know how I'm going to cope doing all that, even for only one day, I feel by doing that all day it would drive me insane. How can I hang on to my sanity if what I am doing is driving me insane? How can I make myself able to bear all that and remain anywhere comfortable. I would need to be a little more comfortable than that, to get through the day without driving myself silly. How do you think I could make myself a little more comfortable?'

'You could try to be more relaxed about it.'

'Yes, that might help, wouldn't it?'

'Yes I suppose it would.'

'Do you think if you could be a little more relaxed about it, you may be a little more comfortable? Don't you want to be a little more comfortable? You know if what you are doing isn't working it is always better to try something else.'

'Yes I suppose that's right. I suppose I should be a little more relaxed. Being uptight isn't working.'

I hope you see, by my pretending to be Yvonne for a day, I made Yvonne see another answer to their problem which may result in her being more comfortable. I had made her change her own truth about her only way to cope with James, by asking her to help me be her for a day. I had, also, to make James see some of his 'truths' were also not helping the situation. This case is not solved yet, but at least everyone involved is making changes and both James and Yvonne have said they have more faith in my ability to help them than anyone else they have seen. This means the rapport is there and it's up to me to find ways to help them both to change so that they can meet in a better relationship than they ever have had. May I quote the Gestalt prayer which says,

'I am I, You are You.
I am not in this world to live up to your expectations.
You are not in this world to live up to mine.
I do my thing, you do your thing, and if by chance we meet, it's beautiful.'

Hopefully that is what both Yvonne and James will do when we have finished.

Hopefully we may learn by our mistakes.

I would like to describe a case which I lost at the very beginning because of my failing to recognise the patient's expectations of what I would do, and secondly by my over enthusiasm to help him. I could see exactly how to help him but had failed to see his 'truths' would not let me help him in that way. Ian Woodlands phoned to make an appointment

but insisted on speaking to me. He was obviously embarrassed to deal with my receptionist. I suppose I should have
recognised this as a sign of his resistance, not of his
embarrassment. When I spoke to him he asked me if I could
help him with his impotency. I told him, as I always do with
every patient, I treat people not symptoms. I went on to say
that I had helped some people with his problem, but I
wouldn't know if I could help him until we met. I added that
nothing works for everyone and one therapist could not help
everyone. He made an appointment.

When he arrived I took him to the therapy room and asked
him to tell me as much about his problem as he could. He
said that about ten years ago he had started to have difficulty
in getting an erection. He said he also had had difficulty in
keeping his erection when he was with a woman. This
problem had steadily got worse until the present time, now
he didn't dare to try anything at all because he couldn't feel
anything, any arousal at all. He wasn't married, but had a
girlfriend who he may like to marry but wouldn't dare to
marry with this problem. At first he said he didn't know why
he should be like this, because he had been alright, without
any bother, before all this had happened. Then he asked me,
'Do you think you can help me?'

I asked him if anything was happening when he first found
he was having difficulty and again at first he said he couldn't
think of anything. I asked him if he had ever suffered from
depression as that sometimes leads to this kind of difficulty.
He admitted he had and at one time before this happened he
said he had seriously considered suicide. He added that that
was all over now and he couldn't think of any reason to be
like he was as everything in his life was going well at the
moment, apart from his sexual problem. He said he had been
to his doctor who had examined him and told him there was
nothing wrong with him and that it was all in his mind. Ian
agreed that may be so.

I asked him to tell me what were his thoughts when he was
going to see his girlfriend. He answered, 'I think I'd better
not start anything with her I won't be able to do. I avoid all
sexual contact. My girlfriend says there's nothing wrong

with me so why be frightened? It's awful, I want to, but I'm too scared.'

I asked him to hang on a little, **'How do you think 'I'd better not start anything with her I won't be able to do.'?'** I explained the fact that to think we had to use our senses, **'Which sense do you use to think what you have just told me?'**

At first he didn't know, but he eventually said, 'I say to myself, 'I won't be able to make love.''

'When you arrive at your girlfriend's how do you stop yourself thinking about making love to her?'

'I just stop myself from thinking about it, I will not be able to do anything anyway.'

'How do you think that?'

'I just say, don't think about it.'

'What is saying to yourself, 'don't think about it,' telling your mind about your ability to make love?'

'I'm saying I won't be able to make love.'

'Yes you're programming yourself to be impotent before you have even tried, aren't you?'

'I suppose so, but I know from experience that I won't be able to do anything.'

'You know from past experience that you have had difficulty in the past, but you can't know what you are going to do in the future unless you programme yourself to fail. Do you want to fail?'

'No of course not.'

'Let me show you how to programme yourself to win.'

'How can I? I don't have any dreams about sex and I never get an erection, even in the mornings. I can't even masturbate myself.'

He really had suppressed all his sexual feelings. I should have recognised it, and thought, 'What is going on in his mind?' However I was so sure I knew how to help him, because of my beliefs, that I taught him how to do a slide change with the things he was saying to himself. The first slide was his home as he was about to leave to see his girlfriend. As he went to the door he was saying to himself, 'I had better not try anything sexual.' He was to change this slide immediately he made it for a picture of himself leaving the house saying to himself, 'I am looking forward to seeing my girlfriend, I find her so attractive.' I asked him to do that six times as quickly as he could, after which he said, 'I make the second picture all the time now.'

I misinterpreted what he was saying, and just said,'G-ood.'. I then went on to teach him to do a slide change of when he was with his girlfriend. The first slide was of his girlfriend smiling at him while he was saying to himself, 'I mustn't think of making love.' He was asked to quickly change this to a slide of himself with his girlfriend, hugging and kissing each other, looking as if both were enjoying it, while he was saying to himself, 'I do love her very much.' After he had done it six times he said, 'I just make the second picture.' I again misinterpreted what he was saying.

Then he said, 'I should tell you this. My father has two wives. Years ago my mother wanted me to marry one girl but my stepmother wanted me to marry another. I didn't marry either of them. My stepmother was so disappointed in me she said she would see I didn't ever enjoy any girl again. She had something to do with a witches coven and I think she put a spell on me. It was about that time I began to have difficulty sexually and was very depressed.

He hadn't said anything about this when I asked him at first about what was happening when he first started having difficulties. I asked him to tell me exactly how he found out about the curse his stepmother had put on him.

He said, 'She didn't say anything to me but she told someone who she knew would tell me what she had done. It was then I started with my difficulty. I am free from her now, I don't believe in it now, but I am still impotent.'

I asked him to close his eyes and imagine he was sitting in a cinema somewhere in the middle of the theatre. While he was waiting for the film to start he was to take his mind out of his body to the back of the theatre where it could watch his body in the middle of the theatre, watching the film which was about to start. The film was in black and white and was of his stepmother telling him to marry the girl she wanted him to marry. He refused and his stepmother putting a curse on him and he then having difficulty in getting an erection. Then I told him to freeze the film and see his body get up from the middle of the theatre and walk up to the screen and step right into the film and as it did, for the film to change into a colour film. He was then to see the film start up again, but this time it was running backwards, everything was in reverse, right back to the beginning of the film. Just like rewinding a film. [See next chapter on reverse film technique for phobias].

I then asked him to do the reverse film again by himself but to see it as quickly as he could. When he had done this I did a film change with him about his stepmother's curse. The first picture was his girlfriend looking sexy and him saying to himself, 'It's no good I am cursed.' This picture should then quickly be changed to another picture of him and his girlfriend making love with him saying to himself, 'It's so good being free to do what you want.' When he had done this six times I asked him if the second picture kept coming in automatically, he said he made the second picture first and had to try to make the first picture after but the last time he just made the second picture. I asked him if he had done this with the other two slide changes and he said, 'Yes. He had done all three slide changes the wrong way. It's important that you show your mind which way you want to go and he had shown it the opposite way to go. When I explained this to him he said he had been to the hospital and seen a specialist who had told him he was physically fit and it was all in the mind. The specialist had told Ian he should get his failure out of his mind. He had also seen another hypnotist who had tried a guided fantasy exercise to relax him. In this exercise the hypnotist had asked Ian to picture himself in a peaceful valley with a stream and birds etc. Ian said it hadn't worked. Unfortunately Ian's time was up. He said he would like to think it over. He phoned afterwards and said to my receptionist he was disappointed with his session. I had told him nothing he didn't know already, and I hadn't hypnotized him and woken him up so that he couldn't remember all his failures. He didn't want to speak to me.

I had missed his 'truth' about his expectancy of hypnosis.

What he wanted wouldn't have worked but if I had known I perhaps could have explained this to him. He also was doing the slide change the wrong way and I didn't spot this until the last time when it was too late at this appointment to do anything about it. He said he didn't want to come back. I had lost him because of the difference between our 'truths' about hypnosis, and possibly his greater truth about his need to be punished. I hope this has shown you a patient can be defeated in his attempt to change by his own 'truths' even when those 'truths' differ from everybody else's. He knew his difficulty was in his mind and I thought I had shown him how to get it out of his mind. He obviously thought I was just telling him all over again that it was a mental problem not a physical one, as the hospital specialist had told him. The hospital treatment hadn't worked so my treatment wouldn't work either, so he didn't take too much notice of what I was asking him to do and had got it all wrong. I'm sure many patients would benefit from what I did, but not if they think it won't work. Remember, 'I think therefore I am.'

CHAPTER 7

Phobias: How to change them

Let us look at the treatment of phobias. In Chapter 4, 'The techniques for change', I deliberately left out the techniques for changing phobias because I wanted to deal with them in this chapter. Obviously many of the techniques for changing phobias are the same as those used in changing any other behaviours. I thought I would describe actual treatments of some of my phobic patients to demonstrate these techniques.

A case of Dental Phobia
A colleague phoned me about Catherine after he had attended one of my lecture-demonstrations at a post graduate centre. He said Catherine was a very severe case of dental phobia who he found impossible to treat. After telling me he had been to my lecture, he said here was a classical case for me to prove that my techniques work. I told him I didn't need to prove anything and many of the techniques weren't mine but ones I had learned from Richard Bandler and John Grinder and others in the N.L.P. field. However, if he would like his patient to change and become a normal, slightly apprehensive dental patient I would gladly see Catherine and help her to change.

When Catherine came for her first appointment she seemed very apprehensive and fidgety and a little cynical about what I could do for her. She was an attractive 38 year old, well dressed and groomed. Over the years she had become progressively more and more afraid of the dentist.

She said she was a friend of the dentist and found him very kind and gentle, but latterly she hadn't been able to let him do anything in her mouth. The last time she attended had been an absolute fiasco. She had put off her appointment as long as she could and eventually when she had gone, she had been terrified. Even when she woke up on the morning of the appointment she thought, 'How can I get out of going to the dentist?' She couldn't really think of any more excuses and her family said they would take her to make sure she got there. She thought, 'Thanks a lot, for nothing. It's me who has to have the treatment.' She had managed to get herself into the waiting room and could hear the drilling in the other room, which was making her steadily more and more terrified at the thought of having to go into the surgery. When the nurse came and told her it was her turn, she thought her legs wouldn't carry her to the surgery. She was trembling all over. As she sat in his chair she thought she was going to pass out. The dentist tried to talk to her but she couldn't make out what he was saying, she couldn't concentrate on anything but her fear. By the time he asked her to open her mouth she just had to get out of there. She fought her way out of the surgery and left, feeling a disgrace, but couldn't help it.

The dentist had phoned her and told her about me, asking her if she would be willing to come and see me. She thought, 'What's the use.' But she knew she must do something, otherwise she would have a lot of pain and end up with no teeth. After she had thought it over and had been persuaded by her family, she eventually came, escorted by her relatives to make sure she arrived. She had decided to see what, if anything, I could do to help her. She said she could see no point in coming because she was just terrified of the dentist and that was that.

I asked her to tell me exactly how she made herself terrified of the dentist, because quite a lot of people weren't that scared. For instance I said I wasn't that scared, would she teach me how I could be that scared? **'Pretend I am you and I have to do exactly what you would do when you have to go to the dentist, how would I do that?'** Actually she had told me quite a lot already how she does that in her history about the dentists.

'Well,' she said, 'When the appointment card first comes through the post I think 'How can I get out of going?' I will make any excuse not to go.'

'**How do you think that? Do you have an internal dialogue with yourself about not going to the dentist?**'

'Yes! I suppose I tell myself I don't want to go. Then I ask myself what I can do to get out of it.'

'**What is saying all that to yourself telling you about your dental appointment? What is it actually saying about how you feel about the dentists?**'

'I suppose it's saying I'm terrified of going.'

'**Yes it is. Do you want to be terrified of doing something which in the end you have to do?**'

'No of course not.'

'**Then why tell yourself to be terrified? Your mind works perfectly when you tell it to be terrified, it starts to make you panic and think of any way to avoid going. Once you have told it to be frightened nothing can stop you being afraid.**'

'I know! I try to tell myself it will be alright but it doesn't work. I have to think, 'How can I get out of going?''

'**Well that's what you have just told yourself to do, and your mind will help you to do exactly what you have told it to help you do, namely to be afraid and not go.**'

'I didn't realize I was doing that. I thought it was the dentist that was making me afraid.'

'**No, you are telling yourself to be afraid before you have even gone to the dentist.**'

'Yes! I can see that now, since you pointed it out, but I hadn't realized it before now.'

'**What do you do next to make yourself afraid when you finally have to go?**'

'All the way there, I am telling myself I don't want to go. My family know me now and one of them generally has to come with me to make sure I arrive.'

'**What is that telling you about how you feel about the dentist?**'

'It's telling me to be scared.'

'**Yes it is, do you want to be scared? Is it helping you to have dental treatment? Is it making it any easier to go?**'

'No! I see now how I'm making myself scared, I thought it was the dentist.'

'**Thinking it's the dentist, is playing the blame game.**' I explained the blame game to her and said, '**If you blame the dentist you are stuck with your fear, because he can't change. He is the dentist, and has to do whatever he has to do if you want to save your teeth. Many people aren't terrified of the dentist so it can't be him, it must be what you do to yourself that makes you terrified.**'

'I can see that now. I couldn't before you showed me. I can also see the point in coming here now. You know, I have to admit before you explained all this to me I thought what a waste of time all this would be. Now I can see how you are helping me. But how will I stop frightening myself when I have to go to the dentist?'

'**When I have enough information about how you terrify yourself I'll be able to help you stop doing that to yourself. What do you do when you arrive at the dentist's door and ring his bell? He does have a bell that you ring, doesn't he?**'

'Yes I ring the bell and tell myself 'You'll have to go in now.'—I know that's telling myself to be afraid. I didn't know it before. What an idiot I am!'

'**No! most of us do stupid things like that, but when you realize you are doing it, you can free yourself from that stupid behaviour.**'

'Quick tell me how.'

'**I still need to know more, how you frighten yourself silly at the dentist's. If I leave something out you may still make yourself frightened. Most of my job is getting information so that I can help you to see how to change. That information has to be complete so that we don't leave something out and spoil the change. What do you do then, after you have rung the bell and gone into the dentist's waiting room?**'

'I look round and think the other patients don't seem to be as afraid as I am. Yes I know that's telling myself I'm afraid.

But then I hear the drill in the surgery drilling someone else's tooth, and I panic.'

'**What do you do to make yourself panic?**'

'I tell myself that will be me soon. YES I KNOW, that's just telling myself to be afraid of the drill, and I don't want to be afraid of the drill.'

'**Then why tell yourself to be afraid?**'

'You must think I'm crazy.'

'**No! most of us do stupid things. That's why we are all neurotic. Some people can handle it when they do stupid things and put it right next time. They are the happy neurotics. Once you have set up a programme and it's up and running you have to wait until the next time to put it right. You have to pre-programme yourself to be different the next time.**'

'Quick then, pre-programme me.'

'**In a minute. What do you do when it's your turn to go into the dental surgery? When the nurse comes to get you?**'

'I think, OH MY GOD! it's my turn. We do the craziest of things to ourselves don't we? Then when I get in the surgery and sit down in the dental chair and the dentist wants to give me an injection, I think, OH NO! not an injection. That's telling me to be afraid of an injection. I do the same when he starts to drill. If I can get through all that I am exhausted afterwards.'

'**Now I think I can help you to pre-programme yourself. I just need to know one more piece of information. If you were cured, no longer afraid of the dentist, could have your dental treatment done without all this fuss, how would you see yourself when you are in control? Would you really feel different about yourself being in control and not letting the fear control you?**'

'Oh! yes I would be much less ashamed of myself, it would be wonderful.'

'**Pretend you are that person now. Close your eyes and see if you can picture that changed person. See how good you look, being in control, no longer afraid. How does that feel?**'

'Marvellous!' there was a broad smile on her face. I knew

she could see the changed self, and it looked good to her.

'Good that's all I need to know. Now close your eyes and picture you are walking into a cinema and find a seat somewhere in the middle of the theatre and just nod your head when you have done that.' She nods her head. 'Good now just imagine you can take your mind out of your body and take your mind to the back of the cinema where it can watch your body in the middle of the cinema, watching the film which is about to start. The film is in black and white and it is about you waking up in the morning and looking at your appointment card which tells you you have to go to the dentists today. You are fussing about and asking yourself if there is any excuse for you not to go. Now you are being taken by one of your family and ringing the door bell. The dental nurse is showing you into the waiting room and you are sitting down looking at the other patients. You hear the drill in the next room and the nurse comes and asks you to come into the surgery. You go into the surgery and the dentist drills a tooth and afterwards you go out of his building exhausted. Now stop the film and open your eyes. Did you manage to do that alright?'

'Yes, just, it was difficult, but I think I managed to do it.'

'Good! now do that again, by yourself this time, as quickly as you can. Remember your mind is watching yourself from the back of the theatre, while you are sitting in the middle of the theatre. The film is in black and white and nod your head as soon as you see in the film yourself leaving the dentist's building. When you come to the end and stop the film, keep your eyes shut.'

After about a minute she nods her head.

'Now while the film is stopped, see your body get up out of the seat in the middle of the theatre and go up to the screen and step right into the film, but as it does the film changes to full colour. Start the film again but this time make it go backwards, from going out of the building, back to getting up in the morning, like re-winding the film, everything goes backwards. Even the voices talk backwards, everything is in reverse. Run it backwards as quickly as you can and when you have done that open your

eyes.'

When you look at something, which you have been afraid of, from another perspective, in this case backwards, your fear of it disappears and you feel nothing about the original thing. I always think, however, that it is always better to over-do the treatment than risk leaving something out. Perhaps missing a trigger which may spark off her fear, so I followed the reverse film by doing a series of slide/film changes.

The first film change I had her do was to see first a film in black and white, of her bedroom and the appointment card saying she had to go to the dentist while she heard herself say to herself, 'How can I get out of going? This film was to be changed as quickly as she could, to a film of Catherine waking up in the morning and saying to herself, 'What a lovely morning, I am so pleased I will be able to go to the dentists today and get my teeth seen to. It really is good to know when you have a healthy mouth.'

I asked Catherine to do this slide change eight times, counting for her as she did it and opening her eyes after each time. The first time she did it she was asked to miss one word off, 'How can I get out of going' from the first film, then the next time miss off another word, and so on, until the last time she only said the words in the second film.

Then she did a film change of ringing the dentists door bell. In the first film she saw the door and bell while she said, 'Oh my God!' In the second film she saw herself at the door saying, 'When I come out I will be so pleased with myself, because my mouth will be healthy.' She did this change four times, missing off another word from the first film each time, until she just said the words to herself in the second film, on the fourth change.

Then Catherine did a film change of the waiting room. In the first film she saw the room with other people in it while she was saying to herself, 'It will be my turn soon.' In the change film she saw herself in the waiting room with the other people happily talking to them and saying to herself as the nurse came to get her, 'Oh good, it's my turn now.' She did this change seven times until on the seventh time she only said the words from the second film.

Then Catherine did a change of sitting down in the dental chair. The first film as she sat down she said to herself, 'Oh! what is he going to do now?' In the change she said to herself, 'How wonderful it will be when he is finished and my mouth is healthy.' She was not in the first film herself, but was in the second in full colour, as in each of the previous film changes. By not actually being in the first film, the patient dissociates from it, but when they are in the second changed film they associate with it. She did this change nine times so the last time she only said the words from the second film as in the previous changes.

Then Catherine did a change of having an injection to numb her tooth. In the first film she saw the needle coming towards her mouth as she said, 'Oh No! not the needle.' In the second film she saw herself having the injection and saying to herself, 'Oh Good! I won't have to feel anything now.' She did this change six times.

Then she did a change of having her tooth drilled. In the first film she saw the drill coming towards her mouth and heard the drill running while she said to herself, 'Oh NO! not the drill.' In the change she saw herself having her tooth drilled and heard the drill running while she said to herself, 'Good that will get rid of all the bad tooth.' She did this change six times.

Then finally Catherine did a change of walking out of the building having had her treatment. In the first film she saw the exit, saying to herself, 'Thank GOD that's over. I feel terrible.' In the change she saw herself going out feeling marvellous, feeling very pleased with herself for being totally in control of herself. Just like the self she had seen earlier, when I had asked her to picture the changed self. She only heard herself singing a happy song. She did this change eight times.

After each of these seven film changes, I tested Catherine by asking her what happened if she tried to just make the first film. In each case the second film came into vision, automatically, before she could complete the first film.

I then took Catherine into my consulting room and had her

sit in my dental chair. I passed her the drill and asked her to hold it over the basin. I started it running and she played the water jet on the drill into the basin. She said, 'I would normally be shaking all over by now but I feel fine.' I thought I could hear her singing as she went out.

A case of Doctor Phobia
Dr. John Pearson phoned me shortly after he had attended one of the courses I had run on hypnotherapy, to ask me if I could help his wife Edith. Edith had unfortunately been diagnosed as having breast cancer and she had to go and have some therapy at the Newcastle General Hospital. The therapy wasn't particularly pleasant, so it would be reasonable for anyone to be a little apprehensive about going to have the therapy. It would also be a little worrying to be diagnosed as having breast cancer. However, in spite of having been a nurse [or perhaps because of it] and also in spite of being married to a doctor, Edith was, unfortunately, absolutely terrified of doctors. Not of doctors socially, but of having to have anything done to her by doctors. She had avoided going to the doctor, as much as she could, ever since being a small child. Now she had to go to the hospital to have her cancer treatment she didn't see how she was going to get there. It seemed to her an impossible task to have to go fairly regularly to have treatment.

I had helped Edith's daughter some years ago with a problem so I had met Edith and she did believe in me as someone who may be able to help. That was a start anyhow.

When she came I remembered her from the time she had brought her daughter. Edith is a very loving, warm, intelligent lady, quite attractive, in her early fifties. She appeared calm and composed, on the outside, anyhow. She must have been O.K. on the inside or it would have shown somehow. Her husband John had come with her so that may have accounted for her calm appearance.

She told me she had been terrified of going to the doctor as long as she could remember. Or it may have been after she had had to go to hospital, as a very small child, to have a minor operation. She said, 'I can remember it very clearly. I didn't want to go but when my parents took me, I was taken away from them forcibly. I was told off for crying. Everyone seemed very aggressive and bossy. I didn't like any of it. I remember when I was taken to the operating theatre everyone was in green and the doctors and nurses were cruel. I cried and screamed when they gave me the anaesthetic and I hurt afterwards. I think that is where my phobia of doctors started from.'

I asked her, **'When do you have to go for treatment to the hospital?'**

She answered, 'Tomorrow.'

It didn't give me much time. I then said, **'When were you last at the hospital? You must have been fairly recently to have the tests done.'**

'Yes I was there, only last week, and I was terrified, even when it was only for tests. I just can't see how I'm going to go tomorrow, when it's for treatment.'

'How do you actually see yourself not being able to go tomorrow? Let me explain first. In order to think anything, you have to use your senses.' I went on to explain how I had gone to Scotland a few weeks ago and when I lay down in the bed I had said to myself, **'I will never be able to sleep in this bed, it's too soft'** [See Chapter 3, page 37]. **'Whenever we think or feel anything, we have to see something, then feel it, or have an internal dialogue with ourselves, then feel that. V-)K/A-)K.** What do you do Edith, to see you can't go to the hospital tomorrow? You probably see something, as that is what you are saying [see the end of the previous paragraph], or you may see something, then say something to yourself, then feel it. V-)A-)K. Teach me to be as afraid of going to hospital as you are. Tell me how you do it.'

'It's the hospital, it just makes me feel frightened.'

'No it's not the hospital. I'm not bothered when I go to hospitals. You must do something with one or more of your senses to make yourself afraid of hospitals.'

'I don't know what I do. I wish I could tell you.'

'O.K. then pretend it's tomorrow, shut your eyes and pretend you are just waking up tomorrow and thinking

about going to the hospital. What are you thinking?'

'I'm thinking Oh! I don't want to go. I'm saying to myself I don't want to go, and I can see the hospital entrance. It doesn't look nice.'

'How doesn't it look nice? It's just a way in, like any other way in. How do you make it not look nice?'

'I suppose I say to myself, I don't want to go in, that's how I don't like it.'

'If you have to go in, what is the point of telling yourself you don't want to go, even before you get there? Does telling yourself you don't want to go make it easier or harder to go?'

'It makes it harder.'

'Yes it does. So what you say to yourself, even before you get there, makes you afraid, not the hospital. Do you want to be afraid? Is it easier to be afraid?'

'No of course not.'

'Pretend you are going into the hospital now. What are you thinking?'

'I'm thinking how can I get out of here?'

'What is that saying about being there?'

'I don't want to be there.'

'Why don't you want to be there?'

'Because I'm afraid.'

'No, you are afraid because you don't want to be there. You are telling your mind that you don't want to be there so your mind is giving you an excuse for not wanting to be there. It's making you afraid. It's your mind that makes you afraid, not the hospital, because you tell your mind to make you afraid. Why do you do that?'

'I don't know, I wish I didn't.'

'Do you really wish you didn't make yourself afraid? Would you think better of yourself if you didn't do that to yourself?'

'Oh yes! Much better. It would be wonderful.'

'Good! Pretend you have been changed and shut your eyes and picture that changed you, who isn't afraid. How does that you look?'

'Great!'

'Good make that picture bigger and more colourful and more real to you. How does that look now?'

'Fantastic!'

'Keep that picture in your mind, because I want you to see it all over again in a minute or two. But before we do that what I need is a little more information about how you make yourself afraid of the hospital. When you get inside the hospital what do you do then?'

'Well, when we are in the waiting room I wish I could get out. I must say to myself, 'I wish I wasn't here.' I know, I'm telling myself I don't want to be there, so my mind makes me afraid. I didn't realize all this before you know, I thought it was the hospital.'

'What happens then?'

'Well, some bossy person comes along and makes me go where ever I have to go and I don't seem to be able to take it.' Her eyes fill with tears.

'Well I think we have enough to make you that 'Fantastic' person now. Shall we do it?'

She looks relieved, 'Yes please!'

I then asked her to do a slide change of waking up in the morning. The first slide was of her bedroom as she got out of bed as seen from her eyes, saying to herself, 'I don't want to go to the hospital.' The change is a film taken be someone else, so that she is in this slide and is of herself getting up in the morning, saying to herself, 'What a beautiful morning to be able to go to the hospital to start making myself healthier.' She did this change nine times, leaving another word out of the first picture until the last time there were no words in the first picture at all. [As in the Dental Phobia, before this one].

I then had her do a slide change of entering the hospital. In the first picture she saw the hospital entrance as out of her eyes, while she said to herself, 'I don't want to go in.' The change slide was a picture of her entering the hospital, saying to herself, 'It's good to be getting on with my treatment, so that I will be better soon.' She did this one seven times, again leaving a word out of the first picture, each time she did the change, until she said nothing in the first slide.

She did a slide change of the waiting room. The first picture of the room only saying to herself, 'I wonder what they will do?' In the change she sees a picture of herself in the waiting room, saying to herself. 'Good it will soon be my turn to get better.'

She did a slide change of the nurse coming for her, for the treatment. In the first slide she saw the nurse and heard herself saying. 'Oh God! it's my turn now.' In the change she saw herself going with the nurse while she was saying to herself, Oh! good it's my turn now. It's good to be getting on with it at last.' She did this change seven times until she said nothing in the first slide.

Then we did a double mirror change. In the first mirror behind her she saw a black and white picture of herself getting smaller like a little girl. Frightened of everything the doctors were doing, feeling alone. In the mirror in front of her, she saw a full colour picture of herself as an adult, like the picture of that 'Fantastic Self' she had imagined earlier. Pleased to be getting on with her treatment to get well, friendly with the doctors, who really were her friends. She started to smile as I asked her to step right into this mirror and be that 'Fantastic Self.' After all the slide changes and after doing the double mirror five times, she found that the second picture and what she was saying to herself in the second picture, came automatically into mind, even if she only tried to make the first picture.

I then did a reverse film of the whole scene. I asked Edith to imagine she was sitting in the middle of a cinema waiting for the film to start. As she was waiting, she was to take her mind out of her body to the back of the theatre, so that her mind was watching her body watch the film. The film was in black and white and it showed Edith getting up in the morning, then going into the hospital and waiting in the waiting room. Then a nurse came up to her and took her for the treatment. At this stage the film is stopped and her body gets up out of the seat and goes up to the screen and steps right into the film. The film changes into colour and the whole scene runs backwards. Everything is in reverse and the film ends as Edith is going backwards into bed.

Edith phoned the next day, late afternoon, to say she had been to the hospital for her treatment and she hadn't been afraid at all. She could hardly believe it. She said the treatment wasn't particularly pleasant but she couldn't get over how brave she had been. I told her as the treatment had to be repeated a number of times, to do a change slide of the treatment. In the first slide to see the treatment as it really was. In the second to see it as making her well and healthy, so that she could look forward to having it to make her well. If you have to do something find a way to enjoy it.

A case of Agoraphobia

Mrs Maria Hindmarsh was referred to me by her doctor. [See his letter to me, below].

Dear Geoff,

> re. Mrs Maria Hindmarsh
> 3 Sheep Hill Road.
> Middlesbrough.

Many thanks for seeing this patient, who has a problem which seems to be related to dentistry and I think may benefit from your expertize. I have not induced hypnosis myself to leave the field clear for any technique you think is appropriate.

Yours sincerely,

Thomas Gimble

p.s. Your two books have been very useful. T.G.

Maria is a lovely lady about forty years old. She became afraid to go out of her home after an intravenous injection at the dentist for a tooth extraction. At the dentists she was seated in his chair, the chair was laid flat and a doctor was trying to give her an injection in her arm to put her to sleep to have a very bad tooth removed. She remembers struggling, then nothing until she woke up. She struggled again and had to be restrained until she was fully awake. She remembered feeling terrified and exhausted as if she had been fighting for her life. [She probably had in her dreams, see later explanation in this case history]. When she got home she was no better, she still felt exhausted and half dead. She had bruises on her legs and arms where she had been held down because of her struggling.

The next day, when she was about to leave the house to go to the shops, she suddenly panicked and felt dizzy. She had to go back into the house and sit down. She had quite a few panic attacks after that, in the bus when it was crowded, she had to get off before it was her stop and sit down on a wall. If she was in a shop and had to wait to be served, she panicked. Supermarkets were a nightmare. She used to go to the club with her husband on a Saturday night for a drink and a dance. The first time she went to the club after her extraction at the dentists she became very hot and sweaty, her skin began to tingle. She had to get out of the club, because of a feeling that if she stayed, she would faint. She had only tried to go back once or twice after that, but each time she had to leave.

She saw the doctor who put her on tranquillizers. He also sent her to the hospital and a psychiatrist confirmed the treatment was to put her on tranquillizers. She was on these for two years before she felt a little better. By this time various places had become taboo. She wouldn't even try to go back to the club and most shops were a little difficult, especially if they were crowded. If she went to a cinema, she had to sit on the end of a row next to the exit sign. She had to see her way out of everywhere she went, otherwise she felt very uncomfortable. She wouldn't travel on buses.

She got toothache again and had to go back to the dentist, but when she got to his door she just couldn't bring herself to go in. She went back home and became agoraphobic again. Tranquillizers were again her only way out, but this time they weren't so good at making her feel safe. She took them this time for about six years. Her toothache went away. [She was more frightened of the dentist than her toothache, so the toothache got better]. Her tooth hadn't healed, but she found she could combat the infection and leave a decaying tooth in her mouth without symptoms. It's often amazing how bad a tooth can be without any symptoms being felt by the patient. I saw a patient today who had ten teeth decayed right down to gum level, only the roots were left, without any symptoms in his mouth being apparent to the patient. He did have a stomach ulcer which no doubt would not be helped by the constant swallowing of pus from his infected roots. That's why most dentists like to check teeth frequently.

She got toothache again and this time she made it into the dentists but she had to go back to have the tooth extracted. She never went back. Her toothache went away and her agoraphobia came back. This time her doctor sent her to me.

She was obviously suffering from first line trauma. The visit to the dentist, her struggling to get out, losing consciousness, still struggling to get out when she awoke had obviously triggered off her unconsciously remembered birth feelings. All the other symptoms are classical of first line trauma. She had obviously, now, anchored first line trauma to all the places she couldn't go into. She felt exhausted and as if she was fighting for her life when she awoke after the anaesthetic at the dentist because she had been dreaming she was being born while under the anaesthetic. Anaesthetic can, and sometimes does, blow away primal gates set up to protect the patient from feeling primal pain. At her birth she probably had to fight for her life to get out. The circumstances had triggered the birth trauma off and she then anchored the birth feelings to all the other places. I explained this to her and she said, 'Yes I do get a feeling I have to get out of all those places, or I will die.' I had told her a story and she believed it, so now all we had to do was re-write the end of the story.

We did that by having Maria first of all re-visualize her marathon. I told her that her birth memory was responsible for her feelings and the places that made her have these feelings were only triggering off those memories. Those places were not responsible, her birth memories were what made her afraid. They were in her mind so it was her mind that made her afraid. If she let her mind choose what she had to feel, then it would probably make her feel all sorts of things she didn't want to feel. I asked her if she would like me to show her how to run her own mind. 'Yes Please!'

'When you are running your mind and can please yourself what you feel, will you feel any different about yourself?'

'Oh Yes! that would be marvellous.'

So we did the marathon. She visualized herself being first, in 50,000,000. Swimming along with 50,000,000 and fertilizing the ovum herself. She didn't stop to think if she could make it, she didn't get off to sit down, before she had won. She didn't let her mind drive her. She asked to be here, she drove her mind to win. She could win now, easily, without feeling she was going to die. She was a winner and that should be the memory she could see and talk about to herself. So I asked her to see herself winning and let that image grow into a forty-year-old lady who would win now. **'SEE that WINNER now, make it big, real, bright, MAKE IT YOU NOW, as you are now.'**

As she did that a smile came onto her face, I didn't have to ask her if she could see and feel it. I knew she could. I knew she had done a V-⟩K A-⟩K. with the marathon. There still, however, were some anchors which may trigger off birth feelings so we did a number of 'changes' to collapse them.

I asked her how she made herself afraid, in all those places she felt frightened. As in the first two cases in this chapter, at first she didn't know she was doing anything to make herself afraid. She just thought it was the places that made her frightened. **'Playing the blame game leaves you stuck being afraid. If you blame places for fear and not what you do to yourself in those places, you are stuck being afraid.'** She had an internal dialogue with herself, in all those places, which scared the hell out of her. I made her aware of the dialogue by asking her to imagine she was in them and asking her what she was doing, thinking, saying to herself, picturing. etc.

The first 'change' we did was when she was going out of the house. She did a zoom change for this. The first picture she looked at was the passage to the door out of her home which we zoomed away and as it got farther away she noticed it turned into a baby trying to be born. As the baby was struggling it said, 'I am going to die trying to get out of here.' This picture was zoomed away until it was just a blur and bringing it back it turned into a full colour picture of Maria going out the door, singing a happy song while thinking, 'I wonder what exciting thing I am going to see outside, or in the shops, or in the supermarket, today.' She did this zoom until the second picture automatically took over.

The next 'zoom' was of a supermarket. The first picture was of a supermarket cashout desk with a queue of people waiting to get checked out. This picture she zoomed away saying to herself, 'I must get out before I faint.' The picture, she brought back was in full colour with a sparkle about it, was of her standing in the queue, saying to herself 'Just watch me beat 50,000,000 again.'

We did the same pictures in shops, buses, the club, and the dentists. She did each 'zoom' six times leaving one word after another out of the first dialogue, each time she did the 'zoom', until the last time she only said the full dialogue in the picture which she brought back. When tested she said when she tried to make only the first picture of the 'zoom', the second one zoomed in automatically in each case.

A case of Cancer Phobia

Jerry McGan's wife phoned me to see if I treated Cancer Phobias. I said, 'No I treat people'. She explained she was very worried about her husband who had a terrible cancer phobia. Did I think I could help him? I again said I didn't know, I would have to meet her husband and do some tests to see what we could do, so she made an appointment.

She came with him to make sure he told me everything. She said, 'He is terrible at not letting you know what is wrong with him and then afterwards he says to me, 'I should have told the doctor about so and so, he may have thought differently if I had told him''

They were both very nice people. Most people are when you really get to know them. Jerry was in his middle sixties, retired, enjoyed fishing, young looking for his age, very mentally alert. His wife was a little younger. She must have been a stunner in her youth, she still was very good looking and smart, obviously looked after herself very well. Both of them were very articulate.

Jerry had had this cough and pain in his chest, this feeling that there was something there in his chest. Also he had a similar feeling that something wasn't right in his bowel. He had been to see the doctor who was unable to satisfy him that there was nothing wrong. The doctor referred him to a specialist who also couldn't satisfy him that there was nothing to worry about. So Jerry had been admitted to the Nuffield Hospital where he had had exhaustive tests including a bronchoscope inspection of his lungs and the same up his rear end. They found nothing wrong. They assured Jerry he hadn't got cancer. For a time he was assured but then the doubts came back. He pestered the doctor for another specialists examination. The specialist told him there was nothing wrong with him and another full examination wasn't necessary. For a time he was assured again, but soon his fears returned.

I asked Jerry if a relative had had cancer and it looked as if we had hit the jackpot. Jerry had been a young man serving in the army when he had had to go home on compassionate leave. His mother was dying of cancer. When he had gone away into the army he had been very close and fond of his mother. She was quite a big lady, that is, she was well-made in an attractive way. When Jerry saw her in hospital he got a terrible shock. She was thin, emaciated, looked like death and was very weak. Jerry couldn't believe it. He was horrified and hurt to see her looking like that. She died the next day and Jerry was terribly distraught. Every time he thought of her he pictured her as she was that day, before her death. To a young man, seeing his mother for the first time as ill as she was on that awful day, cancer was a terrible thing. It was cancer that had made her look like that, and Jerry didn't want to look like that, so he was afraid of getting cancer.

He came out of the army and had a very busy and active business life travelling all over the world and forgot about cancer. He still couldn't think about his mother without picturing her on her death bed. Then when he retired and had some time on his hands he thought about cancer again. If he saw anything in the paper or a magazine about cancer he couldn't look at it. It made him feel awful. When he was fishing he never thought about cancer.

He was a high capacity hypnotic patient so we did the marathon with Jerry and told him that the ultimate destination was that some day everybody had to die. Until that day, however, the purpose of life was to become responsible for himself and make the most of his life so that he could raise his consciousness to a higher plane. I discussed his mother with Jerry and how a young man, suddenly faced with the change in his mother, as Jerry had been, would see cancer as a terrible thing to get. Now that he was older he didn't have to think of it at all. He had a good life and had enjoyed most of it, so why not enjoy the rest of it until he died. He had to die of something in the end, but as he was fit and well and not losing weight, why not make each day he was well, a bonus. I had re-written the end of his story, with a better end. I also asked him if he really loved his mother. I knew what his answer was, but I wanted him to say it.

'Yes! She was a great mother. I loved her very much.'

I asked him how she would want him to remember her. **'Would she want you to remember her as she was on her death bed, or would she want you to remember her as she was all the rest of her life with you? Loving you and you loving her?'**

'As she was when she was well.'

I knew that answer also, before I got it, but I wanted him to say it. **'Wouldn't you also rather like to remember her as she was for all of her life, except for that one day? Is it really fair to her if you don't remember as she really was, not as she was for one day in your life? Wouldn't you like to be remembered for your good points when you die?'**

'Yes of course I would.'

'Then close your eyes and picture her in bed in the hospital and see her as she was on that awful day. Now

Zoom it away until it is just a blur and bring back a picture as she really was when you both loved each other, make that picture big and close and real. Give it a sparkle and see your mothers smiling face looking at you and telling you with her look that she loved you. Smile back at her and tell her with your face that you love her. Just because she is no longer with us on the earth, doesn't change that love. It is still as strong as ever and will comfort you for the rest of your life. Feel it.' He smiled and a tear formed in his eye. It was a tear of joy. I then told him to open his eyes. Then I asked him to do that zoom picture six times as quickly as he could, opening his eyes each time he brought the real picture of his mother back. After he had done it six times, he had a compulsion to make the real picture of his mother whenever he thought about her. It seemed a much better way to remember her. His cancer phobia was also under control.

A case of Spider Phobia
Kate was afraid of spiders. She and her husband are very good friends of mine and they lived in a stone built house with some of the internal walls with the stone deliberately exposed. Unfortunately stone walls seem to attract spiders. If ever Kate saw a spider she had to trap the spider under a pan or jar and when her husband came in from work she would tell him to go and put the spider outside. Apart from her fear of spiders, both Kate and her husband are extremely well-balanced, highly sensitive, very artistic and intelligent human beings.

One day when I was visiting them they told me about spiders. My friend said, 'Go on cure her of spiders.' Kate was a good hypnotic subject and went easily into trance when I told her to. I asked her unconscious mind if there was a reason for her spider phobia and to indicate if there was by lifting her finger. [Ideo-motor finger response]. It lifted. It always will unless the person needs to resist, there is always a reason for any behaviour. I asked her unconscious mind to let her know what that reason was and in a few minutes she became quite disturbed. She became more and more frightened and began to say, 'No.'

I asked her unconscious mind if it thought Kate was strong enough at this moment in time for her to know what was disturbing her, and it answered ,'No.'

I calmed her down and said that she could forget everything that had happened during the trance before she woke out if it. I said she could awake as if she had gone to sleep and had a dream, but the dream had been forgotten before she opened her eyes. I then added that whenever her unconscious mind thought she was strong enough to remember the dream, she would just remember it without doing anything about it. She came out of her trance and apologized for dropping off to sleep.

After a while my friend and I went to the pub and got involved with the landlord who insisted we went down into his cellar and share a pint with him. We got back and told Kate why we had been so late in coming back.

She said, 'That's funny I have been thinking of cellars. When I was small my parents used to put me to bed and they sometimes went out to have a drink. One day when they had done that I awoke and wanted a drink of water. I got up and went to the stairs to go and get a drink. At the bottom of our stairs there was a doorway down into a cellar. The door was open and I could see a light from down in the cellar. I went to the door and called out and there was a scuttle down in the cellar and I slammed the door and put the bolt in and went back to my bedroom and tried to go back to sleep. When my parents came back I told them I was frightened because of what had happened in the cellar. They told me not to worry and went to see what had happened in the cellar. Much to their amazement they found a burglar locked in our cellar. They got the police and they took him away. There were lots of cobwebs and spiders in our cellar, do you think that's why I'm afraid of spiders?'

'It could be, let's ask your finger.' Her finger said, 'Yes' I explained as she was a grown lady now, with no other recognizable fears except spiders, she could stop being afraid of spiders because it wasn't really spiders she had been afraid of in the first place. It had been a burglar. If a burglar came into the house now she would tackle him without being too frightened, so she needn't be afraid of spiders any more. She wasn't. A few days after that she let a spider crawl right up her arm without any fear. I had re-written the story with a different end.

A Cockroach Phobia

When I was running a workshop in Scotland I asked for a volunteer who had any phobia that they would like to be cured of. A young lady doctor volunteered. She said she had been working abroad and the cockroaches at night seemed enormous. She said she hated them and even now thinking about them she felt afraid. I asked her to picture one in her mind now by closing her eyes. She closed her eyes and squirmed in the chair. You could see she didn't like doing that. I asked her to make it smaller and see if that looked any better.

She said, 'It only looks slightly better, but I still don't like it.'

I asked her to make it blurred and she said, 'That makes it worse, I don't know where it is if I make it blurred.'

I decided to do a reverse film of cockroaches to see if that would make a difference. I asked her to open her eyes for a minute so that she could dissociate from the picture of the cockroach she had just been imagining. Once you are in a programme and the programme is up and running you have to come out of the programme to re-set it. I then asked her to close her eyes and picture she was in a cinema sitting somewhere in the middle of the theatre. The film hadn't started yet so she was to take her mind out of her body to the back of the cinema and have it watch her body, sitting somewhere in the middle of the theatre, watch the film about to start. With her mind out of her body, watching her body, watching the film, she was dissociated from being in the film. The film was of her walking at night when she was abroad and after a short while she could notice a few cockroaches scurrying about. She saw them clearly in the film which was in black and white. When she saw in the film that she was afraid, she should stop the film and then watch her body go up to the film and step into the still film. As she did so the film changed to a colour film and it went backwards, everything was in reverse right up to where she was walking along without any cockroaches present. Rewind the film as quickly as she could then open her eyes. She opened them fairly quickly. I asked her to run it backwards once more. When she had done that I asked her if she could see a better self, now that she wasn't afraid of a silly little thing like a cockroach anymore.

She said, 'Yes it would be lovely not to be afraid.'

I asked her to change the tense of what she had just said.

'Yes it is really lovely not to be afraid of cockroaches.'

'Good!' then we did a zoom of being afraid and not being afraid.

In the first picture she saw a cockroach running away while she said, 'Thank goodness it's run away.' Then she zoomed it back in full colour with a picture of herself, bright and sparkling with confidence not a bit afraid, saying, 'There's a cockroach, so what!'

We did a zoom of her being driven by a car and then her driving a car. In the first picture as if out of her own eyes, the car was driving her where she didn't want to go, namely afraid of a tiny cockroach. In the zoom second picture, she saw herself firmly behind the driving wheel, driving herself where she wanted to be, not a bit afraid.

I then asked her how she felt if she pictured a cockroach. She said, 'Not bad, I don't know if I really saw one, how I would feel.'

Someone from the audience asked me, 'If you had a matchbox with a cockroach in it, would you be prepared to bring it out and ask Jane to look at it?'

Before I could answer Jane said, 'As soon as I had done the reverse film of cockroaches they looked much smaller. I'm sure I could look at one now without being afraid.' His question had somehow helped Jane to decide.

I just said, **'Yes, it's important to test straight away. If it hasn't worked straight away, it hasn't worked at all. It won't work later if it hasn't worked now, so you may as well know now. I'm sure 'that' has worked now for Jane.'**

When the workshop was finishing Jane came up and

thanked me and said, 'I feel marvellous, better than I have felt for a long time.' When you help someone to drive their own mind they can go to all sorts of good places.

A case of Sickness Phobia

Claudia was referred to me by a friend who had read my other two books. She is a twenty-seven year old mother of one little girl, Carol. Claudia is terribly afraid of anyone being physically sick. She said she couldn't face having another baby while she had this phobia problem. As soon as she puts Carol to bed she starts to worry in case Carol is sick. She said, 'I have been afraid of anyone vomiting since I was about eleven. When I was eleven my sister was car sick while I was in the car next to her. It was awful. Then I went on holiday with my best friend and she was sick in the bed next to me. I remembered thinking. 'I hope she isn't going to be sick' and then she was, right next to me. Then when I was about fourteen my bedroom was next to the toilet and I remember vividly my father being sick all night in the toilet. The sound of him retching was horrible. I put two pillows over my ears but I could still hear it. Then my sister got the same bug and she was sick in the toilet. If ever my husband is ill I just can't stand it. You don't know how awful it is to be like this. Whenever Carol is sick I can't stand it. That's why I wouldn't have another child, I just couldn't go through it again. I watch what everybody eats just in case they might be sick, it's terrible.'

'**How do you do that? I have seen a number of people being sick and I don't particularly like it, but it's really no big thing with me. How do you make such a big thing out of it?**'

'The sight of it just turns my stomach. It's so messy and lumpy and just horrible, I hate it.'

'**You hate the sight of it, when you see it, do you?**'

'Oh yes. I hate the sound of being sick, that turns my own stomach as well.'

'**So the sound also makes you feel ill does it?**'

'Yes, it's horrible.'

'**What are you doing to your mind by telling yourself that** the sight and sound of being sick is horrible? What is it telling your mind about the way you feel about someone being sick?'

'It's telling my mind it's horrible.'

'Yes, but if something is horrible how are you going to feel about that something? Are you going to feel O.K. about it, or are you going to be scared about it?'

'Oh, I'm going to be scared about it.'

'Great! So you tell your mind to be scared about someone being sick, so your mind says O.K. I'll make you feel scared. Your mind works perfectly, it does everything you tell it to. Only you tell it to do the wrong thing. Do you really want to be scared every time someone is sick?'

'No of course not! I am also scared of someone being sick even when they aren't being sick, just in case they are.'

'Oh great! So you pre-programme yourself even before they are sick just in case they are. How do you do that?'

'I think I picture them being sick, with sick everywhere dripping off the quilt onto the carpet.'

'Oh, that's just great! so you scare yourself silly by making pictures of people being sick even when they are alright.'

'When you put it that way I suppose I must. Silly isn't it?'

'It seems that way to me. How would you like not to do that?'

'That would be wonderful, but how do I do that? I went to the doctor about this and he sent me to a psychiatric psychologist who saw me about six times, but it didn't do any good. I didn't feel any better, so he told me to stop coming.'

'Ah! but he obviously didn't know anything about changing people, or you would be better. Would you really feel better about yourself when you are not bothered about sick?'

'Yes, I would feel much better. I would be free. My life would be so different, I wouldn't have to worry all the time.'

'Good! So close your eyes now.' I had seen Claudia was a very visual person by the way she moved her eyes when she was talking. She was making visual images all the time, her eyes kept looking upwards so she was obviously making visual images inside her bio-computer. When she had closed her eyes I said, **'Now pretend you have been cured and make a picture of that better, freer, you, when your life is so much better.'** She began to smile, so I knew she could see it. **'Give that picture a sparkle. Make it really colourful and close and with a sharp image.'** She almost burst out laughing.

'I must be serious.'

'No if it looks that good enjoy it, wallow in it. It's O.K. to feel smug about it!'

'Oh! it does feel much better.'

'Good! now keep that picture in your mind and open your eyes.' I was going to have Claudia do some slide changes so I explained the principle of the projector with the slide bar. She understood what she had to do. The first slide change was a visual one. The first picture was as if it was out of Claudia's eyes. When she had closed her eyes she saw Carol being sick in her cot with the sick going everywhere. The pictures were in black and white. [I had asked Claudia, before, if she was watching a film on the T.V. in black and white and the same film was in colour on the other side, which side would she watch? She had said the coloured one]. The change was in full colour and was taken by someone else so that Claudia was in the second picture. It was a picture of Claudia lifting Carol out of the cot and saying, 'It's alright, dear, I've got you. Don't worry.' The Claudia in the changed slide is the 'cured' one she had been looking at before with a sparkle. The one who wasn't bothered about sick. Claudia did this six times opening her eyes after each change.

Then I did an auditory change with Claudia. She found it difficult to imagine the sound of someone retching, so I made the sound myself for her while she did the change. We did this change, when she had closed her eyes, by Claudia seeing Carol being sick in her cot and the sick going everywhere while I made a retching noise. While this was happening Claudia said to herself, 'Oh! that's horrible.' She saw this picture in black and white. As soon as she had done this as quickly as she could she made the changed picture and at the same time let me know she had made the change by lifting a finger. This was my signal to make another retching noise. The second picture was in full colour of Claudia lifting Carol out of her cot saying, 'It's alright, pet, I've got you. Don't worry.' The Claudia in the second picture was the cured Claudia who isn't afraid of sick. When she had done this six times, opening her eyes after each change Claudia said, 'I can't see the first picture at all now, the second one is there as soon as I try to make the first one.'

I explained, that was what should happen. I asked her, **'Which picture did you prefer?'**

And with a smile all over her face she said, 'The second.'

I then did a change with the smell of sick. As soon as Claudia tried to smell sick she cried, 'Oh! it's awful, I can't bear it.' Her face was also showing she couldn't bear it. So I decided to collapse the anchor of the smell. I asked Claudia if she minded if I touched her hands and she said, 'No.' I then asked her, while her eyes were shut to imagine the smell of sick and while she did this I pressed the back of her hand with my finger. I asked her to open her eyes and pressed the back of her hand with my finger. Nothing happened. I hadn't caught it at the right time with the anchor. I asked her again, this time with her eyes open, to imagine the smell of sick and it was much easier to see the height of her disgust with her eyes open, her eyes showed it. When she went a little pale and her eyes showed disgust I pressed the back of her hand with my finger. I told her to stop making the image and again pressed her hand with my finger. This time the anchor worked. She went pale and her eyes showed disgust. She said, 'How did you do that? I smell sick.'

I told her about anchors. I then asked her to imagine a smell that she really liked and when her eyes showed pleasure I pressed the back of her other hand. Then I tested this anchor and it worked. So I then asked her to imagine the smell of sick again and as soon as I saw her going pale I fired both anchors together. She looked at me quizzically and said, 'It has no smell now, why can't I smell it?' I explained that as I had fired both anchors she couldn't smell both something nice and an awful smell, at the same time. So the anchor for the smell of sick is collapsed. It won't bother you now. She did a slide change of the whole thing again but adding in the second picture herself saying, 'I'm so pleased the smell of sick doesn't bother me any more.'

Claudia had driven herself to see me in a car, so I asked her how she felt just after she had passed her test and the examiner had given her the slip of paper to say she had passed. She said, 'Marvellous, I could have given him a hug.'

'What did that piece of paper mean to you?'

'It meant I could go anywhere, I was free.'

'How would you feel if I gave you a piece of paper to say you are free of being frightened of sick?'

'Wonderful! I would feel like giving you a hug.'

'Good! I'll settle for you being cured.'

She went out smiling and I'm sure she looked as if she was walking ten feet tall.

CHAPTER 8

Case histories

Let us now look at some case histories in more depth and see how they fit into the the theories discussed in this book.

The first case I would like to share with you is the young lady I mentioned in Chapter 4, pages 59-60. I will call her Eve. I received a letter from Eve's mother about ten days before her first appointment with me. The letter is shown in full, below.

Dear Mr Graham,

Eve Johnstone: Appointment Thursday, 20 Aug. 1987 at 2.00p.m.

My doctor, Brian Jones, arranged the above appointment with you for my daughter earlier this week, for which I thank you.

I felt I ought to drop you a line or two to explain the background to this problem we have, to give you some idea of what is at stake. I know that some professional people prefer not to know the background, but to make their own assessment of the situation. However, the problem has now become so critical that I must impress upon you the seriousness of the situation.

I asked my doctor, 'Who is the foremost leading specialist in the north who would be recommended by the Society of Medical and Dental Hypnosis?' and your name was given as the best. I do hope you are and that you can help us.

Briefly, the situation is that Eve [whose name is really

Anne] has gradually over a period of about 4 years, convinced herself that she is ugly, a second class citizen in everything life has to offer. She has changed the colour of her eyes by buying coloured contact lenses, she has painted round the outside of her eyes to try to alter the shape of the eye sockets, she has bleached her normally fair hair white and has changed her name - all in an attempt to be someone different.

Something may have happened in her life to cause this [this is where I hope you can help]. I have been divorced twice and it could be all my fault. I have even thought it could be something left over from a previous existence [something which has been suggested to me as a possibility—I do not know whether this is something in which you believe, I don't know what to make of it].

You are not the first person we have consulted. I wish you were. We seem to have been passed from one person to another. Some have been very kind and eager to help and I am afraid others have done more harm than good. We have seen a so-called hypnotherapist in Leeds who did not seem to be able to hypnotise anyone. We have seen the local area Psychiatrist and various minions and have latterly been attending Leeds Royal Infirmary to see a specialist there. The latter, although very kind and good is not moving things along fast enough for us now.

I am afraid that last week things really took a turn for the worse. I stayed off work to sit with Eve. She was trembling with fear, her heart was pounding and she said her skin prickled—all I am told signs of terror. She said she could suddenly see no future for herself, that she would be better off 'out of it' and save everyone close to her from any more worry on her behalf. She confided in a close friend of mine that she could see no point in living any longer. I was so worried. I now carry her tablets with me everywhere I go, and only leave her enough for her immediate needs.

Do you think you can help us? I thought that if you could put her 'under' and find out the seat of her problem, and even perhaps suggest to her at the same time that she had nothing to worry about, that she had as much right to be on earth as anyone else and that her physical features were fine, we could perhaps find some peace for her.

I do hope you can help us. I hate to put all the onus on you at this late stage in the treatment. I keep telling Eve that if she can just last out until the 20th Aug. I am sure she will get the help she needs, but with each person she sees her hope seems to diminish. I promise you I have not over-dramatized the situation - we really need some expert help.

We look forward to seeing you.

Yours sincerely,

Mrs Jane Johnstone.

When Eve arrived with her mother, for her appointment, she was dressed in blue denim, with a blue and white polka dot head scarf. Jutting out from the headscarf were some straggly wisps of white hair. She wore very large dark sun glasses, in spite of the fact that the day wasn't sunny or even bright. These glasses completely covered her eyes.

Eve was 25 years old, about five feet eight inches tall, medium build and looked, from what I could see from the outside of her dark glasses, very nervous and apprehensive. When we went into my consulting room she waded into me with, 'I hope you can help me to get my eyes changed. You see they do not show my real self. They are evil and green. Green is evil. I must have an operation on my eyes to change their shape, otherwise people will never see the real me.'

This gave me an ideal opportunity to ask her to take off her glasses so that I could see her eyes. If you can't see your patient's eyes you will miss so much. The eyes are a person's windows onto the world and show many inner feelings and emotions. Without being able to see them it's like trying to find something small in the dark. So I just asked her if she would mind taking off her glasses so that I could see for myself how her eyes looked to me. At first she hesitated and said, 'Are you sure you really want to see them?'

I said, **'Yes I'm sure, if I don't see them how am I going to know what you are talking about?'**

She said, 'Alright! but I warn you, you won't like it.' She

gingerly took them off.

When she took them off I could see clearly why she wore the glasses. Her eyes were a mess. She had applied a red make up all round her eyes which reminded me of a cadaver [dead body used for dissection, remembered from my student days]. The red all round her eyes made her look ghastly, haggard, hollow-eyed and made the rest of her seem pale by comparison. It covered about one inch all round her eyes and somehow made the eye look very unreal. At least it did to me. At this stage I just said, 'I see.' I didn't want to invalidate her truth at this stage, as I'm sure many other therapists had and at the same time lost her by making her think they didn't understand her problem. Remember Descartes said, 'I think therefore I am', If the patient thinks she looks less evil looking like something out of the dissection room, to her, that is the truth, no matter what your truth is, or how much it may differ from hers. If you contradict her belief at this early stage you lose her and no rapport will be established. You can't do anything to help them then, when there is no rapport.

She made various faces indicating, 'I do look awful, don't I?' I just said nothing and put on a poker-face, so as not to give away what I really thought about her eyes. What I really thought was, **'What a mess,'** I didn't think they looked evil.

So I asked her **'What is your real self then, if your eyes don't show it?'**

She answered, 'I'm really much more loving and kind. My eyes show an angry, cruel, evil self, not the real me. But people won't know me if they see my eyes as the are.'

I thought, **'If they see you with the red muck on your eyes they are going to think Good God! what a mess.'** I kept my poker-face on so as not to show what I was really thinking. I also had learned what she was thinking inside. She had just told me she was angry, with cruel, evil thoughts and wanted to change them to kind, loving thoughts. I must admit at this stage I wondered if she was psychotic and I made a mental note to discuss this case with a psychiatrist friend. I knew she was suicidal and thought that was the most pressing thing to deal with at this time. I did a hypnotic capacity test and a resistance test and found her to have a high hypnotic capacity, but with an enormous resistance. This is what I had expected from her interview so far. There was even a little hostility in her attitude to me, or that's what I perceived, anyhow.

[I did discuss her, afterwards, with a psychiatrist friend who said, 'You seem to be making progress so why don't you carry on and if you need help, or feel you get out of your depth, then you can refer her to me at the hospital. I'm sure we won't be able to do any more, or even as much, for her at the hospital than you are doing for her now'].

While Eve was in a light trance, I reminded her of the marathon race she had swam to be here, with all the reasons why she had as much right as anybody else to be on this earth. [See Exercise 1 Chapter 2]. I went on to discuss the only ultimate end to the journey of life, namely we are here to raise our consciousness to a higher plane or we are just recycled to do it all over again. [see my first book 'How to become the Parent You never Had']. Remember also that her mother had said she thought all this may be related to a previous life event, in her letter to me, so presumably they had discussed it and she would most likely accept this concept. I asked her if she wanted to do it all over again, and if not would she like to work at raising her consciousness this time round?

At the end of this interview I asked her if she thought she could work with me? I thought and told her, I could work with her but it is equally important for her to feel she could work with me, as it would really be her who, in the end, would make herself better with my help. I asked her to go away and read my first book so that she would have some idea how I worked and also have some idea of the sort of cases I had worked with in the past. I find my books are most useful for this purpose, as they are deliberately written in simple language that anyone can understand. I wanted her to think about it because of the hostility which I thought I had sensed during this first interview and told her if she decided to come back she should make a few appointments at weekly intervals, so that I could see her fairly frequently at first.

She didn't come back for two months, so obviously she had had her doubts too. It's important to get any doubts sorted out in the beginning and the patient must want to work with you otherwise a great deal of time can be wasted.

When she did eventually come back the first thing I did was to do an O.B.D. test [see my first book, and Glossary at the back of this book]. She was O.B.D. positive and I showed her the exercises I wanted her to do to correct this. [Peter Blythe tells me they have now modified the O.B.D. exercises and the theory so anyone wanting to know about that should contact Peter or David McGlown in Chester]. During this visit Eve discussed her early childhood where she saw herself as a small girl about 9 years old with short fair hair and green eyes. The green in her life seemed to turn everything evil. There were green fields all around where she lived. There was green outside the nursery school she went to when she was very small. She could remember feeling bad about green as early as that. Green made her hate herself and feel stupid and afraid of becoming independent. Once again I thought I sensed hostility towards me, or perhaps towards any change I may want Eve to make in her life. I hadn't discussed any changes I wanted her to make at this stage, so I knew I would have to play it cool or I would lose her. On the next visit Eve discussed her fear that she may lose control if I hypnotized her, to find out what was making her life the way it was. She thought if she was deeply hypnotized she may lose herself and disintegrate into nothing. She stated she always had to keep firm control of herself. I just said, **'Bullshit! you are out of control now. Who do you think you are kidding? Do you really think being so unhappy is being in control? I don't. Would you like me to show you how you can control your mind much better than the way you are trying to control it now?'** She didn't drive a car but her mother had driven them to my consulting rooms, so I asked her, **'How long it would take you to get home after you leave my rooms, if you take every second left hand turn on the way home?'**

After a while, with a puzzled look on her face, she said, 'We would never get home.'

'No you wouldn't would you. If you took every second left hand turn you would just end up where you didn't want to be. The way you are controlling your mind you are ending up where you don't want to be. Do you want to be as unhappy as you are now? Wouldn't you like me to show you how you can drive your mind so that you end up being happier than you are now?'

'Yes please!'

At last her resistance had lowered and for the first time I didn't sense any hostility. She had told me how I had to work with her, at least for now. I asked her to pretend we had done some work already and she was now able to drive her mind to where she wanted to be. I then said. **'Close your eyes and picture this you, in control and being happy, driving your mind where you want, not being controlled by GREEN but able to go and do whatever you want.'** After a short while she began to smile so I knew she could see this self and she liked it more that the self seeking treatment. This is what I needed to know. The patient has to see the changed self as a better self than the one seeking treatment, for changes to be possible. I then said, **'Now make this picture brighter and closer and put some friends with you and hear laughter.'** I knew she saw and heard it, because she was smiling all over her face. **'Make that picture as real and strong as you can,'**

After she had done that I asked her to open her eyes and describe the picture to me. She smiled again and told me she had seen herself dressed in red, laughing and joking with her friends. She added the information that her friends seemed to be able to accept her much more easily. This told me that she found her friends had some difficulty in accepting her normally. I wasn't too surprised at that. While she was telling me about the picture I noticed she was rubbing her fingers with her thumb. I drew her attention to her thumb and said, **'Be your thumb. What is it saying to the rest of you?'**

She stopped rubbing so I told her to do it again and look at it and tell me what her thumb is saying.

She said, 'I do that to comfort myself.'

'No!' I said, 'I don't want to know what you do. I can see that for myself. I want to know what your thumb is thinking about the rest of you, when it does that to you.'

'It's saying get going. Get on with it.'

'O.K. let's do that! Close your eyes and imagine you are standing between two full length mirrors, one in front of you, and one behind you. Turn to look at the mirror behind you and see an image of yourself dressed in dull clothing. See the whole reflection grey, dull, lonely, quiet and frightening. Imagine yourself walking away from that mirror and as you do notice the image getting smaller and younger and less mature. Now turn round and see in the mirror in front of you the picture of yourself, dressed in red, laughing and joking with your friends. Walk up to this mirror and notice you are much more happy, bigger, brighter, more mature, more in control than you have ever been because you are driving your mind. See how your thumb is telling you to get on with it.' [Her thumb was already rubbing her fingers again. I was just pointing it out and reminding her again what it was saying to the rest of her].

Her face was showing me she was experiencing all this because it was brighter than I had seen it to date, so I said, 'Now step right up and into the mirror in front of you.'

'Oh yes,' she said.

'Now open your eyes.'

I had her do this slide change six times as quickly as she could, while I counted for her, opening her eyes each time she completed the change. When she had finished I asked her how she had found doing that.

'It's much easier to see the mirror in front of me.'

'What happens if you try to just picture the mirror behind you now?'

'The one in front comes into view.'

'Does it do that automatically, without you having to make it happen?'

'Yes.'

I discussed what Kierkegaard had said about 'Whenever we translate 'what is' into language or thought we distort 'what is' and then believe that distortion to be the truth. She looked at me and said, 'You mean I am doing all this to myself? I'm making all this up in my head? I wondered if that was what was happening?'

The next time she came she was much more cheerful and reported she had been doing the exercise I had taught her at the last visit. It had made her feel much more positive. I asked her to take off her glasses which she did without hesitation. Her eyes were still painted red, but she didn't mind my looking at them anymore. She said she had felt much better until this morning, when she had had some difficulty in getting the red make up right.

I asked her to tell me exactly what had happened and what she was thinking at the time. Eve said, 'When I was fixing my eyes this morning I couldn't get it right. I was saying to myself, 'No that's not right, you must get it right.' I could feel myself getting uptight about it. I was all hot and bothered.'

'What is telling yourself "I'm not getting it right, I must get it right", doing to you? What is that saying to your mind?'

'It's telling me to be worried and uptight if I don't get it right.'

'Yes! and your mind is then showing you, you are worried by making you all hot and bothered. Your mind works perfectly, you are just telling it to do the wrong things. Do you want to feel all hot and bothered when you don't get your make up right?'

'No.'

'Then don't tell it you must get it right when you are not getting it right. Why is it so important to get it right anyhow?'

'It's as if I have to keep myself inside. The lines are like bars in a prison keeping me in, but I have to be kept in.'

'What do you have to keep in? Is it the colour green? Your eyes are green.'

'I seem to see a green demon inside my head. It's horrible, with a spear. The demon is feeding off me, draining all my strength, and keeping me from thinking the way I want. My eyes show the green colour of the demon. I mustn't let anyone see him.'

We did a slide change of the demon in Eve's head and then a drawing of the demon on the floor and Eve stamping on the demon. I asked her to actually draw a green demon and then put it on the floor and stamp on it. I also asked her to keep on doing the other exercises which were helping her.

The next time she came in she took off her glasses but still had the red make up around her eyes. She reported she didn't get hot and bothered if she couldn't get her make up right, she just told herself she would get it right in the end. I asked her if she had drawn the demon and stamped on him. Eve said, 'Yes would you like to see him?'

I said, **'Yes.'** [See the picture she showed me on the next page]. The demon was green and the umbilical cord was pale red and she explained that was how it was feeding off her, sapping all her strength. She also explained the rooms at each side with padlocks round the doors were other parts of her brain which the demon was controlling. She said she knew that she was responsible for making the picture of the demon, but her need to make it was very strong.

Eve's Drawing of her Demon

She also said she felt much better and was looking for a white wig so that she could go out and meet her friends. I asked her why she needed a wig and she said, 'Well you see I have bleached my hair so much it's falling out and looks terrible.' She had always worn the blue and white polka dot head scarf up to now and I had never seen her hair. I asked her to show me, but she said I wouldn't like her if she did, so I didn't press it this time. I felt it wasn't necessary to see it, at least up to now.

I wasn't surprised she frightened herself by making pictures inside her head, of demons like that feeding off her, so I thought we ought to see if we could do something about him. I wondered who the demon was but thought if we could get rid of him we may not have to know who he was. I asked her to close her eyes and go inside her mind and ask her mind if it would let her know when the demon first came into her mind. I set up an ideo-motor finger response [See my other books for ideo-motor responses], so that her index finger would rise when the answers to my questions were 'yes'. I first asked her unconscious mind if it would help us to find out when the demon first came into her mind. Her finger rose up.

I asked her if the demon was there when she was at nursery school.

Her finger said 'Yes.'

'Was It there when she was getting born?'

'Yes.'

'Was was it there before she was born?'

'Yes.'

'Was it there from a previous life?'

'Yes.'

I thought it was probably saying 'Yes' because she had discussed this possibility with her mother, but it gave me a good excuse to get rid of the demon now. As the demon had nothing to with her present life I asked her unconscious mind if it would be willing to help us to get rid of it from her mind in her present life. Her finger lifted, indicating 'Yes.'

I asked her to make an image of herself walking along a clear pathway. The pathway was going up a tall mountain with mist and clouds round the top. As she walked up the pathway she was to get more and more into this dream and make it seem real. When she reached the top, in the clouds, she could see some large flat stones and sitting on one of the stones she would be able to see a very wise old man. The old man was beckoning to Eve to come close to him and when she was quite close, he took out a small steel chest from behind a stone and unlocked it and opened it up. She could see there was nothing inside and the wise old man told her to put the demon into the box. As soon as she had done that he quickly closed up the box, with the demon inside and fastened all the locks on the box and then wrapped the chains round the box and fastened them with padlocks. He then told Eve to leave the Demon with him, where he would keep him, safely, fastened up in the box forever, unless she should ever need the demon again. If she did need the demon again she could always come back for him. As the demon had nothing to do with Eve's present life, the wise old man said he could see no reason why she should ever need him again. I asked Eve then to return down the mountain to celebrate her freedom from the demon, with all her friends and to make strong pictures of that in her mind. I also asked her to draw the demon locked in the box, so that she could see where he was now. The first picture of the demon still had an umbilical cord attached to her so it was still part of her, I hoped the next drawing would show that his attachment to her was broken.

The next time I saw Eve she said she had had a bad week. She had gone to a wig shop to get herself a white wig, as I explained before, but they didn't have one. They said they could make her one but it would cost about £200. She locked onto never going to get what she wanted and gave herself a depressive time. She said she was pleased to see me and hoped I could knock some sense into her. She hadn't drawn the green demon in a box either. I told her I expected it for the next appointment. I felt it was important for her to imagine the demon outside of her and if he was in the box he couldn't be inside her head. In order for Eve to draw the demon in a box from her imagination, she had to imagine him out of her head.

I discussed what I thought a person really was and it wasn't just what you saw on the outside. A person had a

mind and personality which was much more important than
her outward appearance. Eve had a very strong belief about
her eyes and hair and I had to be very careful not to lose her
by invalidating her belief just yet.

I was delighted with Eve on her next visit and we made a
lot more progress with her belief about her outward
appearance. I explained her belief about her outward
appearance was the crazy part of her mind. The sane part
had made the drawing and really understood what she was
doing to herself. I'm sure she agreed and I didn't lose her at
all. I did a double mirror exercise with Eve and asked her to
draw it for the next time. By drawing from her imagination,
she had to start thinking in the way that would help her to be
more happy. The mirror behind her was for the past while
the mirror in front was for now and the future. When I asked
Eve to imagine the new Eve, happy, confident, with a wide
range of choices about how she looked on the outside,
because she felt good on the inside and then told her to give
that Eve a sparkle about her, she burst into a fantastic smile. I
asked her to hold on to that image and step right into the
mirror. All through this visit she was much more lively. She
produced the drawing below. She said, 'I know I was just

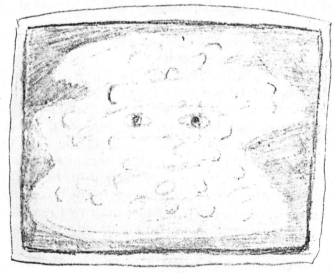

Eve's Demon in a Box

imagining that demon was in my head and he was feeding off me, but somehow I feel that I have got rid of him in that box. [You can see she hadn't given him a umbilical cord so she had imagined the demon without one, to be able to draw it. It doesn't look nearly as ferocious, in fact he looks quite friendly].

On her next visit, Eve brought a picture of herself walking through the mirror. I think she had taken it from a character she had seen in a magazine. She had given herself a white mane which she has been trying, unsuccessfully so far, to buy. She was, however, much more outgoing and even seemed a little happy with herself. She confessed that on her

Eve stepping through the Mirror

first visit she had thought, 'Are you trying to help me or destroy me?' It took her two months and the opportunity to read my first book to decide she would give me a try. She now said she was pleased she had, because she could see a future in living.

In the picture she had a red fitted jacket on. She also brought notes on how she thought of herself before starting treatment and how she saw herself now [See below].

BEFORE Obsessed and dominated by the colour Mid-Green. Eyes especially, small green circles. Constant feeling of being dumb/stupid, through disability to overcome problem in my head that kept the green strong. Insecurity through school made me weaker and the green stronger. All I ever saw was green and a feeling of stupidity, it kept my mouth shut and closed my brain down, programmed only to see green and feel stupid. I couldn't see past it to step into life and be myself. I had always to act to hide what I could see and what I felt, it was so painfully hard to do. It didn't always work, so kids just thought I was strange, a source for fun, made me feel even smaller, gave the green more power-enveloped in green. Felt stupid and condemned to misery for years. *I had never learned what I was really like, couldn't learn properly at school. I had a strong need to socialize but my attempts were defeated and stopped by the programme in my head, I never learned how to socialize. I thought very little of myself because I believed I was what I saw in my head. Whenever I looked at myself I saw the identity of the image in my head. Having green eyes didn't help, especially if you believe that your eyes are your identity, giving me overwhelming reminders several times a day of this image and feeling, telling me how worthless and stupid I was and green. With the added disadvantage of no coordination I could never win. I was helpless and hopeless/ I felt like I had a brain the size of a pea/name/colour of uniform/ place where I was born and grew up/ image in my head/signing my name/ Mrs Green/house colour Yellow. My stepfather's name was Graham. [Perhaps that's what took her so long to make up her mind to come back. She hated her stepfather]. She wrote all this during the week before coming for this last appointment and I'm sure you will be able to see that she is using the past tense in everything she is saying.

It is easy to see which tense she is using above, when you lookat her description of how she feels now.

NOW I feel the colour red is my power now. I am surrounded by red. Red blood is flowing through my veins. I am absorbing red from everywhere. This gives me a feeling of strength—strength of mind—physical strength and will-power. I feel I am starting to develop my own personality properly through red. I feel much more confidence, not afraid to speak up for myself. My strength is from within myself. I want to become a powerhouse of strength, so that if any of those bad thoughts dare to come any where near me they will just rebound straight off. If I find my mind wandering I just think of a large RED strong box in front of me. A person with a Red aura, which I now believe I have has strength of character and I need to prove to myself that I have this. Socializing would be ideal. I have provided myself with a new image, so that I now know what my soul looks like.

She added after I had read this, 'You have a very powerful red aura, I would like to feel like that?'

I said, **'How do you see or feel my aura?'**

'I feel it as waves and vibrations coming from you.'

'Good! Close your eyes and picture the same waves and vibrations coming from you. Can you feel them?'

'Yes I can.' She sounded very excited.

'Excellent! See them getting even stronger and feel them, now. Hang on to those feelings and let yourself feel them always.'

She was smiling all over her face. I explained she had let her mind be a judge, jury and jailer and it had placed her in a cell and thrown away the key. I had given the key back to her. We did a slide change of that. In the first picture, as if out of her eyes, she saw the inside of a prison cell with the door locked. Quickly she changed this picture to one of herself in bright red walking through the open cell door saying to herself, 'It's so good to be free.'

Then we did a picture of this strong, free, happy, confident Eve, holding a little baby Anne. [Eve's name was really Anne before she changed it to Eve]. Eve was looking into Anne's little green eyes and saying to Anne, 'I love you and will take care of you and see you never hurt again.' Little baby Anne was at the same time looking into Eve's big green eyes and saying, 'I love you Eve and will not make you afraid again because you are strong now and can look after me.' [See 'How to Become the Parent You Never Had']. We then repeated the two mirror exercise she had done on the previous visit. Eve looked good as she went out today and I feel confident it won't be long before she is totally the new person she would like to be.

A Case of Stress manifesting in asthma attacks

Andrew Foster came to see me to see if I could help him with a stress problem which expressed itself in his getting asthma attacks whenever he got uptight. He worked in a management position where there was a lot of stress. He worried about his job even when he came home after work and it affected his ability to get to sleep at nights. Often he would lie awake, for what seemed like hours, worrying about work. It wasn't that he couldn't do the work, he was held in high esteem by the directors of his company. He had resorted to using a Prednisone Steroid preparation when his asthma got really bad. He didn't like taking the prednisone because of the side affects. It was causing him to have a pain in his chest over his heart which worried him. It also resulted in his putting on some weight which made him uncomfortable. He found difficulty in getting into and out of his car. He went fishing, but of late he found it more difficult to enjoy even that. He had had hypnosis a few years before coming to see me for a stammer and had found that helped him quite a lot. Everyone was telling him he was doing a great job at work but he felt somehow he wasn't and he would worry about what could go wrong in the future. Nothing had gone wrong but he still couldn't stop worrying. He was a typical example of a person who dreaded something happening in the future, which had never gone wrong yet. [See Chapter 3. How not to use your mind].

He had a high hypnotic capacity and good visualization

with a low resistance. Everything was in his favour for a good result. I saw him once a month over a period of six months. I taught him to do the goal directed meditation, described in my book 'How to Become the Parent You Never Had' to lower his general stress level and the marathon to boost his confidence. He did a split screen and double mirror exercise of the situations in which he may have got uptight, to make him more relaxed and accepting, without lowering his own standards.

I taught him to do a slide change of who was driving his mind and another slide change of going to sleep. For sleep he saw, out of his eyes, the lower part of the bed with his legs turning over and over and the bed clothes all ruffled. Then he quickly changed that for a picture of him sleeping soundly and peacefully.

I taught him to do a slide change to stop eating to excess at the weekends and he did a double mirror exercise for his worry about future problems at work, that probably would never happen. For this he saw in the mirror behind him, himself worrying about things that may, or may not, happen. In the mirror in front of him which he was encouraged to step into, he saw himself happily getting on with his work, paying attention, only, to any problems as they happened. He was to clearly see that he was not just imagining them happening at some time in the future and worrying about that.

He has not needed any prednisone at all over the six months. He is much more relaxed and competent at work. Even his directors have remarked on his improved state of mind. He feels much better in himself and is pleased he came to see me, but doesn't know why he didn't come years ago.

CHAPTER 9

Conclusions

There are only two types of people on this earth, the happy neurotic and the unhappy neurotic. There isn't anyone else. We all from time to time, when something happens that for a moment upsets our equilibrium, are guilty of behaviour which makes the situation worse not better. That's why we are all neurotic. Neurotic behaviour is behaviour which makes a situation worse and farther away from homeostasis. When that happens, some people can recognize what they are doing and halt that behaviour which aggravates the situation and, as it were, go into reverse and make it better. This is applicable both to physical and/or mental behaviour. These people are the happy neurotics because they always have choices available to them to make life more comfortable.

Then there are those people who, when something happens that upsets their equilibrium, start some physical and/or mental behaviour which makes the situation worse and sets it going out of control. These people, however, unlike the happy neurotic, feel impotent to do anything about it. This is sometimes because they don't recognize that what they are doing is making it go out of control, or sometimes, even when they do recognize what they are doing, they get stuck in a particular behaviour and don't seem to be able to do anything else. We call this a 'Stuck State'. This book is about how to help people out of 'stuck states'. These people are the unhappy neurotics, because they seem to have no choice when it comes to their neurotic behaviour and are stuck being uncomfortable.

This book is an attempt to show you first of all how we get stuck and then what we can do to free ourselves from the trap of unhappiness. It's amazing how many people respond to the simple question, 'How are you today?' with a quite negative answer. This answer will begin programming them to feel bad. A typical answer may be, 'Not too bad', which insinuates 'Not Good' either, or 'Alright' with a questioning tone of voice, which insinuates, 'I'm not sure if I'm really good or not.' Another answer may be, 'Fair to middling,' which sounds O.K., but who only wants to be middling? Why not be fantastic? Only occasionally do you hear a really positive answer like, 'Very well thank you,' or 'Fantastic'. When you believe in the statement Descartes made, about the only absolute truth in the working of the human mind, 'I think therefore I am', most people seem to belong to the unhappy neurotic class. What a pity, when it's so easy to be happy, if only you know how. Most people spend much longer learning to drive a car, or simple household gadget, than they spend learning how to drive their own mind. If you don't drive your own mind, it will drive itself at random, generally ending up somewhere you don't want to be. Or worse still, someone else will drive it more often than not to somewhere you don't want to be. So how do you drive your mind?

Before you can feel, or do, or think, anything you have to use one of your senses. You have to see something, or hear something, often an internal dialogue, or smell something, or taste something, then you feel something, or think something, or do something. The process of feeling, thinking, or doing something has to start in your senses. Often this part of the process is unconscious so that a person is not aware of using his senses before he feels, thinks, or does something. Nevertheless it is an essential part of the process to use your senses. The way you use these senses influences to a very large degree what you feel, think, or do. When you know how and this book has been written to show you how, it is a simple task to alter the process in the senses so that you alter what you feel, think, or do. This gives you more choices so you end up a happy neurotic instead of being unhappy. When you change what you think, feel, or do, you change what you are.

Soren Kierkegaard said, 'Whenever we translate 'What is' into language or thought, there is always a distortion of 'What is'. Richard Bandler also said, 'Thoughts and words are only inadequate labels for experiences'. These distortions, or these inadequate labels, are made distortions or labels in the senses. By altering these distortions or labels in the senses we alter what we feel, think, or do, so that we alter what we are. Why spend the rest of your life being unhappy when you can be happy? You are much more use, both to yourself and everybody else, when you are happy.

We alter the processes in the senses by altering the visual, auditory, olfactory, gustatory and kynesthetic variants by which we perceive. When we do, we alter what we perceive and are. The essential ingredient for this to work is the persons emphatic belief that the changed self would be a substantially better person to be. If they don't see this, it won't work. A mind will nearly always do what you tell it to do, provided it's not already in a programme which is up and running. This means provided it is not already carrying out a previous request. It is very difficult to halt and change a mind which is already running. In order to change it you often have to come out of the programme so that you can pre-programme it for a future time. Minds work perfectly, but sometimes we tell them the wrong things to do.

This is very obvious when it comes to people who suffer from phobic stuck states. A person who has a phobia invariably plays the blame game. They blame the phobic situation for their fear. So long as they do this they will remain phobic. It is not the phobic situation that makes them phobic, but what they tell their minds to do about the phobic situation, that makes them afraid. They often pre-programme themselves to be afraid even before they get to the phobic situation. It is imperative to show a phobic it is what he/she is saying to themselves [or seeing in an internal picture] that makes them afraid. Phobic situations have no power to make anyone phobic. Once you can show the phobic person how they are making themselves phobic, it is easy and quick to help them to change.

Always remember every individual is unique and each may have a different way of processing their own thoughts. It is always wise to test first to see how they are processing their thoughts as in exercises 6->9. Every individual has their own truths. When these truths are similar, a rapport will automatically develop as in the relationship between myself and my friend Bill Pemberton. [See Chapter 6]. When they are very different it becomes extremely difficult to communicate and you have to be careful not to end up insulting the other person.

It is very important with all these exercises to show the mind which way you want it to go. If you don't you will only create confusion. [See Chapter 6, last case study].

To become skilful at helping people to make useful changes in their lives it is necessary to both learn the techniques of change and, more importantly, to practise using those skills. You will never learn them from a book or even watching someone else do them. The only way to become proficient is to do them yourself with someone, preferably with a trainer looking on at first and see what happens. Many of the techniques look too easy to be any use and you may have some difficulty in believing they could work. It is only when you see the results that you will find it easy to believe. The techniques take some practice to be able to easily help someone to make the correct pictures to bring about successful changes in themselves. If the techniques don't work either you haven't made the correct pictures to bring about change or you have left something out. It may be that you have failed to collapse some powerful anchor still affecting the patient.

Remember no technique will work with everyone. No therapist can help everyone. When you know a large number of techniques and become a very skilful therapist you will stand a much better chance of helping a large number of people to become happy neurotics. In doing so you will also become a happy neurotic yourself. It will seem like magic. I wish you well in your endeavours to become a happy neurotic . . . why be anything else?

Appendix

VARIANTS IN VISUAL PERCEPTION

Colour	Black and White
Clear	Blurred [out of focus]
Near	Far Away
Bright	Dull
Large	Small
Sparkle	Plain
Foreground	Background
Three Dimensional	Flat
Symmetry	Asymmetry
Movement	Still

As a general rule the variants on the left of this list make the thoughts and feelings of whatever you are picturing, stronger. The variants on the right of this list make the thoughts or feelings weaker. There may, however, be quite a few exceptions to this rule.

Other variants of visual perception are:

Horizontal
Vertical
Perspective
Framed
Unframed
There are always others

These last five and others may make the thoughts stronger or weaker depending on the individual. All of these variants of visual perception, however, will alter the quality of the images being formed and the thoughts and feelings connected with the images.

It is possible to help people who make transparent pictures in their unconscious mind become aware of them in their conscious mind. The start of this process is to make them accept and know that they do make pictures. With training and acceptance they will begin to see more and more in their conscious. The training consists of asking them to keep on making visual perceptions and at the same time asking them, 'How did you do that?' Eventually they will begin to see the pictures in their conscious mind to a much greater extent.

VARIANTS IN AUDITORY PERCEPTION

Urgent	Peaceful
Compelling	Soft
Noisy	Quiet
Important	Unimportant
Immediate	Later
Persuasive	Boring
Wakeful	Restful
Loud	Hushed
Wild	Gentle
Jarring	Rhythmic
Agitate	Soothing
Laughter	Crying

As a general rule the variants on the left of the above list will make the thoughts and feelings connected with the auditory images stronger, but there are always exceptions. The variants on the right will normally make the thoughts and feelings associated with the auditory images weaker. Once again there are always exceptions.

The most common way to feel something is to make a picture then feel it. V->K But sometimes they say it then feel it A->K Sometimes to feel something a person will use a combination of the other senses V->A->O->G->K Visual [see]. Auditory [hear]. Olfactory [smell]. Gustatory [taste]. Kinesthetic [feel]. Each sense image can lead on and stimulate another sense image.

Again like the visual and auditory senses there are variants in the Kinesthetic perception that will strengthen or alter the feelings.

VARIANTS IN KINESTHETIC PERCEPTION

Love	Hate
Hot	Cold
Courage	Fear
Pleasure	Discomfort
Glad	Sad
Comfortable	Pressure
Smooth	Rough
Satisfaction	Hunger
Strong	Weak
Still	Movement
Happy	Unhappy
Possess	Loss

There are always others

As a general rule the variants on the left will lead to a more pleasant feeling and the ones on the right will lead to a more unpleasant feeling. Again there are always exceptions.

The Olfactory and Gustatory senses [Smell and Taste] also have variants but the three most important and frequently used, senses are Visual, Auditory and Kinesthetic. Some smells and tastes, however, do lead to very powerful feelings. e.g. A favourite perfume can have a great effect upon the way a man might feel for a beautiful lady. A warm pint of beer can make a man from the north east of England quite bad tempered. A strong body odour on a man may well be very off putting to a lady.

Glossary

AFFECT BRIDGE: a technique used in regression, where non-relevant remembered feelings of a person are deliberately made stronger to enable the person to go back to a time when those feelings were relevant.

ANCHORS: a set of circumstances often remote from the behaviour but, which nevertheless, has attached to them, and promotes unconsciously a particular behaviour, which may be positive or negative.

BIO-COMPUTER: the living computer which is the human brain.

BLAME GAME: a game we all play, when we blame others or other things for how we feel. Feelings are personal experiences created by ourselves, for which we alone are responsible. If we blame others or other things then to get out of a feeling, others or other things are going to have to change. As this is unlikely to happen, we are stuck and trapped in the feeling, if we play the blame game.

EGO: The self of a person, the esteem with which a person holds themselves.

FUTURE-PACE: Self imagining by a person as to how they would cope in the future with a new learned behaviour.

HYPNOSIS: a state of mind where there is a marked narrowing in the field of concentration with a corresponding increase in attention within that field.

HOMEOSTASIS: a balanced, comfortable position in life.

NEUROTIC BEHAVIOUR: behaviour which generally leads to an increase of a problem and a move away from homeostasis.

NEURO-LINGUISTIC PROGRAMMING [N.L.P.]: A movement started by John Grinder and Richard Bandler to help someone to improve their standard of behaviour and communication towards excellence.

ORGANIC BRAIN DISFUNCTION [O.B.D.]: work done by David McGlown and Peter Blyth in Chester showing that if certain developmental reflexes are not formed during the early life of children, they will suffer a number of physical and psychological difficulties in later life. These refelexes can be formed in later life by a series of exercises which will help the then adult cope better with their difficulties.

PACE and LEAD: N.L.P. terms, meaning to imitate exactly a persons behaviour to establish rapport, then to change your behaviour and see if the other person will follow your lead.

PHOBIA: a fear reaction to a stimulus where the response far outways the imput stimulus. The fear is quite unreasonable by other peoples standards. To the phobic, however, the fear is very real and uncontrollable.

PSYCHOTIC: a classification of a person who is severly psychologically ill. The illness is thought to be genetic in origin, therefore not cureable. It is normally treated by drug therapy to enable the sufferer to cope.

RAPPORT: in psychotherapy, the esteem and trust with which a person holds the therapist. This is an essential element in all psychotherapy.

SCHIZOPHRENIC: a classification of person with a psychotic illness.

STUCK BEHAVIOUR and STUCK STATE: a behaviour over which a person seems to have no choise but to follow the behaviour, whether they want to or not. A stuck state is the state in which a person who has a stuck behaviour finds themselves.

Bibliography

DESCARTES, RENÉ: French philosopher and mathematician [1593-1662]. Educated by the Jesuits. Served in the Dutch and Bavarian army. Moved to Holland 1629 where there was a much greater freedom of speech, where he was more able to work on his philosophical ideas. In his search for the absolute truth pertaining to the working of the mind he came up with his theory expressed in the phrase 'Cogito ergo sum.' [I think therefore I am].

KIERKEGAARD, SÖREN: Danish philosopher [1813-1855]. Studied theology at Copenhagen university. He spent his short life after his father died writing his philosophy. He was the precursor of modern existentialism. One of his theories was that whenever we translate anything into thoughts or words we distort that thing in the process of thought.

KORZYBSKI, ALFRED: Mathematition, philosopher and linguist. Author of 'Science and Sanity': An Introduction to Non-Aristotelian Systems and General Semantics [4th edition]. Lakeview, CT: The International Non-Aristotelian Library Publishing Co. 1958.

BANDLER, RICHARD AND GRINDER, JOHN: Founders of the Neuro Linguistic Programming [N.L.P.] movement. Authors of 'Frogs Into Princes.' Box F, Moab UT: Real People Press 1979. 'Reframing': Neuro-Linguistic Programming and the Transformation of meaning. Box F, Moab, UT: Real People Press. 1982. 'Trance-formations': Neuro-Linguistic Programming and the Structure of Hypnosis. Real People Press 1981 'The Structure of Magic 1' and 'The Structure of Magic 2' Published by Science and Behavior books Inc. Palo Alto, California 1975 and 1976

BANDLER, RICHARD: Author of 'Using Your Brain—for a Change.' Real People Press 1985 and 'Magic in Action' Meta Publications. 1984.

JANOV, ARTHUR: Author of 'The Primal Scream', 'The Primal Revolution', The Anatomy of Mental Illness', The Feeling Child', Primal Man', Prisoners of Pain', 'Imprints. The Lifelong Effects of the Birth Experience'.

SPIEGEL, HERBERT: Author of 'Trance and Treatment', Basic books, New York 1978. See also 'The Inner Source,' Exploring Hypnosis with Dr. Herbert Spiegel', by Donald S. Connery. Holt, Rinehart and Winston, New York. 1982.

ELMAN, DAVE: Author of 'Findings in Hypnosis'. Published by Pauline R. Elman. 1964.

BLYTHE, PETER and McGLOWN, DAVID: two psychologists who were working together in Chester, England and are now working independently on various aspects of psychology and psychotherapy. Contact Peter Blythe, 4 Stanley Place, Chester. CH1 2LU. David McGlown. The B.I.R.D. Centre, 131 Main Road, Broughton, Chester. CH4 0NR

To order a copy for yourself or a friend or patient by mail order send to—

REAL OPTIONS PRESS,
Dunsopp House
Lucy Street
Blaydon upon Tyne.
NE21 5PU
U.K.

....Cut here

Book by the same Author
With self help exercises to help a person mature and become responsible for themselves and therefore have many more options in their lives.

Please send........ Copies of **'HOW TO BECOME THE PARENT YOU NEVER HAD' by GEOFF GRAHAM** ISBN 0 9511951 0 7 to

Name...

Address..

....

....

.... Post Code...........

I enclose £6.95 + £1.05 [post and package] for each book U.K. market.

'IT'S A BIT OF A MOUTHFUL' by **GEOFF GRAHAM**
ISBN 0 9511951 1 5
With self help exercises for Obesity, Smoking, Alcoholism, Oral Sex, Anorexia Nervosa, Nail Biting, Thumb Sucking, Dental Phobia and other Dental problems.

Please send........copies of **'IT'S A BIT OF A MOUTHFUL' by GEOFF GRAHAM** to

Name...

Address...

....

....

.... Post Code...........

I enclose £6.95 +£1.05 [post and package] for each book U.K. market.

....

'THE HAPPY NEUROTIC' by **GEOFF GRAHAM**
ISBN 0 9511951 2 3
With techniques to help a person get out of a stuck state and become more happy.

Please send........copies of **'THE HAPPY NEUROTIC'** by **GEOFF GRAHAM** to

Name...

Address...

....

....

.... Post Code...........

I enclose £6.96 +£1.05 [post and package] for each book U.K. market.

Please send the completed order, with cheque, to 'Real Options Press, Dunsopp House, Lucy Street, Blaydon upon Tyne. NE21 5PU. U.K.

Please Print Name and Address clearly.